To Terry

With Congratulations on a Wonderful
Performance.

Love

Galde.

(The 1996 one!)

To Life!

Royalties to the National Playing Fields Association

To Life!
A Treasury of Jewish
Wisdom, Wit and
Humour

Compiled and Illustrated
by
Topol

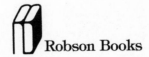

Robson Books

To my Mum and Dad, Rela and Jacob, with
love and admiration

First published in Great Britain in 1994 by Robson
Books Ltd, Bolsover House, 5–6 Clipstone Street,
London W1P 7EB

Illustration and compilation copyright © 1994 Chaim
Topol

British Library Cataloguing in Publication Data
A catalogue record for this title is available from the
British Library

Printed in Great Britain by Butler & Tanner Ltd,
London and Frome

FOREWORD

I was born in 1935 and, when I grew up in Tel Aviv, there was no shortage of playing fields – there were sand dunes as far as the eye could see, though there was little grass or trees. Now, like everywhere else, we have to restrain the developers from covering every piece of land with concrete. We all need open spaces, preferably green ones, for our children and, if we are honest, for ourselves, too, as we grow older.

I am delighted to be following in the footsteps of such illustrious figures as Michael Caine and Dudley Moore, all of who have previously created marvellous books for the National Playing Fields Association. This splendid organization has invited me to put together a selection of Jewish wit and wisdom in the hope that it will help to raise much-needed funds for their fine work.

I would like to make it clear right from the start that I am in no way qualified to compile a comprehensive volume containing the full spectrum of Jewish wit and wisdom through the ages and from all four corners of the world. That would be too vast a task for any one person, no matter how learned. The choice of possible material is literally endless, so all I could try to do is, like someone dipping into a bottomless coffer of treasure, randomly seize a fistful of jewels and, from these, select the ones which most appeal to me.

The process of selection was on the one hand very enjoyable as I went through stacks of wonderful material, but on the other hand, I felt anxious trying to assess the relative merits of a scriptural quotation and a juicy joke, both of which in different ways seemed appropriate to this book. But appropriate to whom? Would everyone understand the humour? Well, when I played *Fiddler on the Roof* for a month in Japan, I was

quite surprised to find the Japanese audience laughing or crying at the same spots as an audience in New York, London or Tel Aviv. I hope, dear reader, that you find this book entertaining. I have included lots of quotations and anecdotes by and about some favourite show business personalities, who happen to be Jewish. And it was such fun drawing their portraits!

The rest of the material may be roughly divided into three categories: scriptural and traditional writings, Yiddish and Hebrew sayings and proverbs, and a pot pourri of what are considered to be Jewish jokes, although I have no doubt that some are told as Irish jokes by the Irish, as Russian jokes by the Russians and by the Greeks as Greek jokes. How come? Because people have something in common no matter where they are: they are all God's children.

ACKNOWLEDGEMENTS

I would like to thank the many friends and colleagues who have passed on favourite stories and anecdotes for inclusion in this book. Their help is greatly appreciated – both by me and by the National Playing Fields Association.

I would also like to thank Elaine Stern and her former colleagues and staff at the Oxford Centre for Hebrew and Jewish Studies who provided so much valuable assistance and material.

I was born in 1962. It's true.
And the room next to me was
1963 . . .

JOAN RIVERS

A man should live if only to satisfy his curiosity.

SAYING

Two kangaroos are talking to each other, and one says 'Gee, I hope it doesn't rain today, I just hate it when the children play inside.'

HENNY YOUNGMAN

'It won't be long now,' said the circumciser to the boy's parents.

If you strike a child, strike him only with a shoelace.

TALMUD

. . . **I** had a Jewish delivery: they knock you out with the first pain and wake you up when the hairdresser shows.

JOAN RIVERS

I was an only child so I was very overprotected. My tricycle had seven wheels . . . and a driver.

RITA RUDNER

A fine and healthy little five year old, the only worry Michael gave his parents was that he had still not uttered his first words. He seemed bright and very responsive, but he just didn't speak.

One day his mother put a bowl of grapefruit segments in front of him. Michael had a taste and immediately spat it out. 'Ugh,' he cried out, 'you shouldn't serve such a bitter and unsatisfactory breakfast. This is absolutely disgusting!'

'Michael, you spoke!' cried his mother.

'Michael! Baby! You uttered your first words! Mazeltov my boy!' said his father.

They hugged their son. They were ecstatic.

After they had got over their surprise Michael's father said to his son, 'Michael, darling, why have you never spoken before? How come you're so articulate? Such long words, my boy. But why no word until today?'

'Well,' said Michael, 'until you gave me this grapefruit the food's been wonderful!'

When I grow up I want to be a little boy.

JOSEPH HELLER

Before Mrs Kaplan sent her son off for his first day at school, she hugged him and said, 'Good luck, my bubeleh. Be good, be nice, bubeleh, and work hard. And remember, bubeleh, at lunchtime eat all your food and play nicely with all the other children. Oh, my bubeleh, I'm so very proud. Remember, bubeleh, Mummy loves you *very* much.'

That afternoon, when little Kaplan returned home, his mother cried, 'Bubeleh, my bubeleh, give Mummy a hug! What a beautiful bubeleh you are. So, tell me, what did you learn at school today?'

'Well,' said the boy, 'I learned that my name is Joshua.'

A grandmother was playing in the park with her two small grandchildren when an old friend came along.

After the usual greetings, the friend said, 'And these must be your grandchildren. How old are they?'

'Well,' replied the proud grandmother, 'the doctor is four and the lawyer is two.'

When I was a kid, I had no watch. I used
to tell the time by my violin. I used to
practise in the middle of the night and the
neighbours would yell, 'Fine time to practise
the violin, three o'clock in the morning!'

HENNY YOUNGMAN

*A*dolescence is a kind of emotional seasickness. Both are funny, but only in retrospect.

ARTHUR KOESTLER

I was born in Miami Beach . . . I know that's where most people die!

RITA RUDNER

The Finklebaums were determined that their children Charlotte and Peregrin should have a proper 'English' education and sent them to top public boarding schools.

One day Mr Finklebaum was phoned by the headmaster of little Peregrin Finklebaum's school.

'Hello, Mr Finklebaum, I'm sorry to have to call you at work, but we are sending Peregrin home for a few days. I'm afraid we have had to suspend him.'

'My Peregrin, *suspended*, what has he done?'

'It's rather a delicate matter . . . um . . . Peregrin has been caught playing with his genitals.'

'Headmaster, I never realized you were of the faith!' replied Mr Finklebaum.

'I don't understand what you mean, Mr Finklebaum.'

'Headmaster,' laughed Mr Finklebaum. 'Some of our best friends are genitals.'

If I do not acquire ideals when young, when will I? Not when I am old.

MAIMONIDES

If you don't respect your parents, your child will not respect you.

MAIMONIDES

Disciples increase the teacher's wisdom and broaden his mind. The sages said, 'Much wisdom I learned from my teachers, more from my colleagues, from my pupils most of all.' Even as a small piece of wood kindles a large log, so a pupil of small attainment sharpens the mind of his teacher, so that by his questions he elicits glorious wisdom.

MAIMONIDES

Education is that which remains when one has forgotten everything one learned in school.

SAYING

When we are young our parents run our life; when we get older, our children do.

VICKI BAUM (Austrian–American Jewish Writer)

——————❦——————

As a boy I was ashamed to wear glasses. I memorized the eye chart, and then on the test they asked essay questions.

WOODY ALLEN

There are four kinds of disciples:
Quick to learn, but quick to forget. In him the gift is cancelled by the failing.
Slow to learn, but slow to forget. In him the failing is cancelled by the gift.
Quick to learn and slow to forget. His is a fortunate lot.
Slow to learn and quick to forget. His is an evil plight.

TALMUD

'Jeffery Katz,' asked the teacher, 'what is three per cent?'

Jeffery shook his head. 'You're right,' he replied. 'What's three per cent?'

The most aggravating thing about the younger generation is that I no longer belong to it!

ALBERT EINSTEIN

I dated a 21 year old. Took her to my apartment. Put on a record of Charlie Parker and Dizzie Gillespie playing a Cole Porter tune. She thought it was classical music.

WOODY ALLEN at 40

Mr Levy was delighted at the wholly unqiue fashion in which he planned to celebrate the bar mitzvah of his oldest son.

'A safari!' he explained. 'I have arranged for an air flight to Africa. The bearers are hired, the jungle trails chosen, the guide obtained. It will be completely novel. We will go there, listen to native chants, shoot at some wild game. Standing on the body of a dead lion, my son will recite his prayer in Hebrew, there will be services, and we'll return here for the champagne. How's that?'

The invited guests were ecstatic over the sheer enormity of the bad taste involved. On the appointed day, all were flown to Africa. The bearers were lined up and the guide led the way. The guests, all in appropriate costumes down to pith helmets and mosquito nets, threaded their thrilling way along the trails through the rain forest.

Suddenly, the column came to a halt and the guide called out, 'There will be a delay of one hour.'

'Why?' demanded Levy indignantly.

'What can I do?' said the guide, 'There's another bar mitzvah safari ahead of us on the trail.'

ISAAC ASIMOV

*M*y mother loved children – she would have given anything if I'd been one.

GROUCHO MARX

There are only two things a Jewish mother needs to know about sex and marriage:
1. Who is having sex.
2. Why aren't they married?

DAN GREENBURG

When a young man marries, he divorces his mother.

SAYING

What's the difference between Jewish and Italian mothers?

The Italian mother tells her child, 'If you don't eat up your food I'll kill you.'

But the Jewish mother tells her child, 'If you don't eat up all your food, I'll kill myself!'

How many Jewish mothers does it take to change a light bulb?
None. 'Don't worry about me, I'll sit here all alone in the dark.'

Mrs Moskowitz was bursting with pride.

'Did you hear about my son Louie?' she asked Mrs Finkelstein.

'No. What's with your son Louie?'

'He going to a psychiatrist. Twice each week he's going to a psychiatrist.'

'Is that good?'

'Of course it's good. Forty dollars an hour he pays, forty dollars! And all he talks about is me.'

ISAAC ASIMOV

'After all our troubles with Johnny, he's now such a wonderful boy. He gives father and me such naches,' said Shirley.

'You had troubles?' asked Miriam.

'And how! After his first week at University, Johnny told us he'd "come out of the closet!" '

'Oh no!' cried Miriam. 'Aren't you and Stanley upset?'

'We were,' replied Shirley. 'But Miriam, is he going out with a nice Jewish doctor!'

'My Sheldon is under therapy,' said Mrs Bloom.

'Why?' asked Mrs Cohen.

'Lord knows,' replied Mrs Bloom. 'Apparently he's got an oedep . . . p . . . ee . . . I remember . . . it's an oedipus complex.'

'Oedipus, schmoedipus . . . just so long as he loves his mother.'

Mrs Gold: My boy is a professor, no less, of law at Cambridge University.

Mrs Levene: Well, my boy is the top brain surgeon in the North of England *and* President of the Medical Association.

Mrs Rosen: *My* boy, now, he's a Rabbi.

Mrs Bloom: A *Rabbi!* What kind of career is that for a Jewish boy?

A young Jewish actor phones home: 'Mama, Mama, I'm so excited. I've got the part! I'm playing the husband!'

Mama replies: 'So you couldn't get a speaking part?'

MAUREEN LIPMAN

The Lord could not be everywhere, so he created mothers.

SAYING

My obstetrician was so dumb that when I gave birth he forgot to cut the cord. For a year that kid followed me everywhere. It was like having a dog on a leash.

JOAN RIVERS

It was Katy's birthday, and her mother gave her two scarves – one green, one orange.

On the Sabbath, Katy wore her best dress, topped off with the contrasting orange scarf, and went round to her parents' house.

Her mother took one look and said 'So, you don't *like* the green scarf?'

When little Isaac passed away at the age of seven, all his relatives and family friends cried bitterly at the graveside. His mother, of course, was distraught.

'Isaac, Isaac, how could you leave me? Tell the Almighty how miserable we are. Isaac, tell the Almighty to see to it that your father at last finds a job to support your brothers and sisters. Isaac, Isaac, *beg* the Almighty for your sister Rosa, who is already twenty-six and still hasn't got a husband. Isaac, *please* tell the Almighty that I have terrible problems with my kidneys and ask him to cure me. Isaac, Isaac, also tell the Almighty to cure my sister Sarah's arthritis, she can hardly walk. And Isaac, ask the Almighty . . .'

At this point the gravedigger became impatient and interrupted her: 'Mrs Greenberg, with so many problems to sort out, you shouldn't send a child – you should go and do it yourself.'

Mrs Levene picks up the telephone:
– Hello?
– Mama, Mama, I'm in a terrible state.
– Darling, bubeleh, what is it?
– Oh Mama, we're all snowed in, the car
won't start, the children might have measles,
I've got a cold, the house is a mess, I've got
no milk and, worst of all, I've got twenty
women from the shul coming over for
dinner. Oh Mama, Mama, what am I going
to do?
– Don't worry, sweetheart. Mama will sort it
all out. I'll get the train and two buses and
will walk the two miles from the bus stop to
your house. On the way I'll buy some milk
and food for tonight. I'll put the children to
bed, clean up the house and make a nice
meal for your friends. Don't worry –
everything will be OK.
– Oh, Mama, thank you, *thank* you. But what
about Dad? What will he do?
– Dad? What dad? Your father's been dead
for two years.
– Is this 72592?
– No, this is 72692!
– Oh no! Does that mean you're not coming?

A sign in a pet shop window caught Jacob Levine's attention. It read:

THIS MONTH'S SPECIAL: A YIDDISH-SPEAKING PARROT

Jacob couldn't believe his eyes. He walked into the shop and asked the assistant, 'Is that sign a joke? I don't believe it! I've never heard anything so funny.'

'It's absolutely true,' said the assistant, 'I swear. Here, come and meet Yankel the parrot.'

Jacob addressed the parrot in Yiddish:

Jacob: Sholem Aleichem.

Parrot: Aleichem sholem!

Jacob: You really speak Yiddish?

Parrot: Yes, I speak it fluently.

Jacob: Well, I'm very pleased to meet you. I'm Jacob Levine.

Parrot: I'm Yankel the parrot.

Jacob: So, where are you from?

Parrot: Originally Poland, but we moved to the East End years ago. I lived with the Fishberg family for many years. Then I had my bar mitzvah . . .

Jacob: How marvellous. I can't wait for you to meet my mother.

'So,' Jacob said to the salesman. 'You've answered my prayers. I've been looking for a companion for my mother, one that speaks Yiddish. I'll take the parrot. How much do you want?'

'£2000,' replied the salesman.

'£2000?!' gasped Jacob. 'I can't afford that sort of money. I'll give you a thousand.'

'Sorry, sir, no deal. This is a very *very* special parrot indeed.'

'£1500 then.'

'Well, I don't know . . . oh, all right then, it's yours for £1500.'

'It's a deal,' said Jacob. 'And if you could wrap it up and send it to my mother in a pretty box with a bow . . .'

'No problem, sir,' replied the salesman.

The next morning Jacob phoned his mother. 'Happy Birthday Mum!' he said.

'Thank you, bubeleh. And thank you for that brilliant present. Such an unusual idea.'

'Mum, you really liked it?'

'Darling, I loved it . . . it was absolutely delicious!'

'Delicious!' shrieked Jacob. 'Mum, that parrot spoke fluent Yiddish. His name was Yankel.'

'Oh Jacob, you're such a comedian,' laughed his mother.

'A comedian!' yelled Jacob. 'That parrot cost a lot of money. It was from Poland and lived in the East End. We spoke to each other in Yiddish.'

'You're crazy, Jacob. Maybe you're working too hard.'

'I'm not, Mum. I swear, it's true.'

'OK, Jacob,' replied his mother. 'But if he could talk, why didn't he say anything?'

Receptionist:	Good morning, Mr Thompson's office. How can I help you?
Caller:	I'd like to speak to my son, please. It's Mrs Rabinowitz.
Receptionist:	Mr Thompson, it's your mother, Mrs Rabinowitz.
Mr Thompson:	Mum, how are you? Why didn't you come to our flat-warming party? Such a wonderful flat and my own mother is too busy to see it. Charlotte and I were so disappointed . . .
Mrs Rabinowitz:	Hello there, Hyman. That's a beautiful building you live in.
Hyman:	What? You saw the building?
Mrs Rabinowitz:	Sure. I was there from six until eleven.
Hyman:	So why didn't you come up?
Mrs Rabinowitz:	I forgot your name!

A giant wave swooshed onto the shore and swept Joshua into the sea. Mrs Cohen went berserk and cried out, 'G-d! G-d! I know we don't go to shul as often as we should, I know we don't keep kosher outside the house and I am really sorry. But please give us back our little boy. Please, *please* G-d!'

Suddenly, a miracle occurred as yet another wave swept Joshua back onto the shore.

His mother rushed up and grabbed her son. As the Cohens wrapped Joshua in towels to dry him off, Mrs Cohen held up her hands to the blue sky.

'So, G-d,' she said, 'Where's his hat?'

Danny Finkle returns to his home in Golders Green, three years after emigrating to Australia.

'Danny, Danny,' cried his mother. 'Where's your beard?'

'Ah, Mum, no one has beards in the surf club!'

'But you still go to synagogue on Shabbas?'

'Everyone works on Saturdays. It's my busiest day!'

'But surely you still keep kosher?'

'Nah – that Australian pork is the best!'

'Danny,' gasped Mrs Finkle. 'Tell me, are you still circumcized?'

Two Jewish mothers meet in the delicatessen.

'So, Gertie, how are the children?' asked Angela.

'To be honest with you, my Brandon has married a hussy. She stays in bed all morning, poor Brandon has to take her breakfast in bed and, when she gets up, she spends all his money at the shops. Even worse that that, when he gets home from work, there's nothing on the table to eat. She drags him out to the most overpriced restaurants. My poor Brandon.'

'Shame,' replied her friend. 'And what about Brandon's sister, Sarah?'

'Ah, now, *she* has married an angel. He brings her breakfast in bed, gives her all the money she needs to go shopping and in the evening he won't let her cook, but wines and dines her in the most expensive restaurants in town!'

A Jewish gangster was dining at a kosher restaurant on New York's Lower East Side when members of the mob came in and pumped him full of lead. He crawled out of the restaurant and stumbled up the street to the tenement block of his childhood. With his hands clutching his bleeding stomach, he crawled up the flight of stairs and banged on the door of his mother's flat, sobbing, 'Mama, Mama.'

The old woman looked at him and said, 'Bubeleh, come in. First you eat, then you talk!'

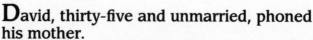

David, thirty-five and unmarried, phoned his mother.

'Mum, it's me, David. I'm calling from New York. I've got great news.'

'David, you're in New York? What's wrong, are you ill?'

'No, Mum, I'm great. Guess what?'

'You've been promoted?'

'No, even better. At last I've met the future Mrs Schonberg.'

'A wife?'

'Yes, and Mum, she is *gorgeous*.'

'Marvellous! Harry, come here! David's going to get married, . . . at last!'

'Hang on a second, Mum. There are a couple of things I should tell you before you meet my fiancée. I know this might be difficult, but she's not Jewish.'

(Pause) 'Ah . . . well, it's not the end of the world. We all need someone, I suppose, especially at your age. Harry, she's a *shikse*!'

'Your very understanding, Mum. She's not of our colour either.'

'A *shvartze*? Harry, she's black. David, so your children will have a good skin colour. Anyway, if you're happy, then so are your father and I.'

'What a mother you are! Just a couple more problems. Layla doesn't have a job and I've been made redundant, so we're going to come and live in England. The problem is, we don't have any money and we'll have nowhere to live when we come back.'

'So you'll both live here. You and Layla can have our bedroom and Dad will sleep on the sofa.'

'But Mum, what about you? Where will you sleep?'

'Don't worry about me, darling. As soon as you've put down the phone, I'll be putting my head in the oven!'

*M*rs Goldblatt in Fortnum and Mason's food department is approached by a liveried floor manager in top hat and tails.

'May I be of assistance, Mrs Goldblatt, Madam?'

'Gimme a qvarter of chopped liver.'

'Certainly, Madam.' He calls out – 'A quarter of a pound of our best French pâté de foie gras for Mrs Goldblatt. Thank you. Will that be all?'

'I vant a half a pound of worst.'

'Certainly, Madam – a half a pound of our finest German salami for Mrs Goldblatt. Will that be all, Madam?'

'No – I vant you should gimme a box lockshen.'

'With pleasure, Madam. A box of our best quality Italian vermicelli for Mrs Goldblatt – and will that be everything, Madam?'

'Dat's all I vant.'

'Thank you. And would Madam like it delivered or will you schlepp it home yourself?'

MAUREEN LIPMAN

*T*he benefits of wine are many if it is taken in the proper amount, as it keeps the body in a healthy condition and cures many illnesses.

But the knowledge of its consumption is hidden from the masses. What they want is to get drunk, and inebriety causes harm . . .

The small amount that is useful must be taken after the food leaves the stomach. Young children should not come close to it because it hurts them and causes harm to their body and soul . . .

The older a man is, the more beneficial the wine is for him. Old people need it most.

MAIMONIDES

A drunk gets a red nose from white wine too.

SAYING

When a poor man eats a chicken, one of them is sick!

SHOLEM ALEICHEM

Groucho once offered a toast to the hostess, a prominent socialite. 'I drink to your charm, your beauty and your brains – which will give you a rough idea of how hard up I am for a drink.'

What does a Jewish Princess make for lunch?
Reservations!

Bernie and Seymour sat down in the kosher restaurant. The waiter came over.

'Nu, what d'ya want?'

'A glass of orange juice,' replied Bernie.

'An orange juice for me too,' said Seymour, 'but make sure the glass is clean.'

The waiter went away and came back with two glasses of orange juice. 'So,' he asked, 'who wanted the clean glass?'

The day after the Rosens' dinner party, Gillian Leibowitz phoned up her hostess.

'David and I had a wonderful evening,' gushed Gillian. 'And those profiteroles were so delicious, I had three!

'Four, actually,' replied her friend, 'but who's counting?'

Five things were said of garlic:
It satisfies your hunger.
It keeps the body warm.
It makes your face bright.
It increases a man's potency.
And it kills parasites in the bowels.
Some people say that it also encourages love and removes jealousy.

TALMUD

Mmmm ... that was delicious! So can you eat any other part of the animal?

MARILYN MONROE after eating her first matzo ball

A person should not speak at meals lest his windpipe act before his gullet and his life become endangered because of it.

TALMUD

Asked whether he was a vegetarian for religious or health purposes, the Jewish writer, Isaac Bashevis Singer, replied, 'It is out of consideration for the chicken.'

———————🦌———————

. . . She's so fat, she's my two best friends. She wears stretch kaftans. She's got more chins than the Chinese telephone directory.

JOAN RIVERS

A man went into a kosher restaurant. The waiter came over to serve him.

'To start with, I'd like some borscht and then . . .'

'Sorry, sir,' interrupted the waiter, 'but we couldn't get any beetroot to make the soup.'

'Never mind, just give me some chopped liver.'

'Just served the last portion!'

'Okay, I'll have roast chicken.'

'We're out of chicken!

'Salt beef?'

'Surprisingly, we didn't get the delivery of salt beef,' replied the waiter.

'For G-d's sake!' exclaimed the man. 'Just bring me a cup of tea and a piece of cheesecake.'

'Wow, sir,' gasped the waiter. 'An appetite like yours, I've not seen for years!'

Look not on wine when it is red, and
sparkles in the cup.
It may go down smoothly:
But at the end it bites like a serpent,
And stings like an adder.

PROVERBS

A man went into a kosher deli. He sat down and ate his dinner. When he had finished, the owner walked up to the table.

'Was everything all right, sir? Did you enjoy your meal?'

'Lovely, thank you,' replied the man. 'Except for one thing. I would have liked more bread with the soup.'

The next night the same man returned to the deli. This time the owner asked the waiter, 'How many slices of bread did you give that man last night?'

'Two slices.'

'Tonight,' said the owner, 'you give him four slices with his soup.'

After the meal, the owner approached the diner.

'How was your meal tonight, sir?'

'As good as last night's,' came the reply. 'But I really would have liked more bread with my soup.'

The next night the man returned and asked for the same order as the two previous evenings. Once again the owner asked the waiter how much bread he'd given the man the night before. This time the owner told the waiter to take a whole loaf of bread, cut it down the middle and give the gentleman both halves.

After dinner, the owner came over to the man and asked, 'Was everything all right, sir?'

'Yes, fine, thank you,' replied, the man. 'But I see we're back to two pieces again.'

During the filming of *Guys and Dolls*,
Samuel Goldwyn asked the Jewish
choreographer Michael Kidd whether he
liked Jewish food.

'Yes, of course I like Jewish food,'
answered Kidd.

'You like Lindys?' enthused Goldwyn. 'You
eat kneidlach, kreplach, chicken soup . . .'

'Yes!'

'Let's go down there.'

As they walked to Lindys, Goldwyn
rejoiced in his favourite Jewish delicacies –
kneidlach, kishke, gefilte fish, lockshen,
kugel . . .

'They have lovely Jewish food here. I love
it all. So,' he asked the waiter, 'what's the
speciality today?'

'Irish stew.'

'Good,' replied Goldwyn, 'that's what we'll
have.'

Eat a third and drink a third and leave the remaining third of your stomach empty.

Then, when you get angry, there will be sufficient room for your rage.

TALMUD

*D*esire is the very essence of man.

SPINOZA

It is natural for a man to woo a woman, not
for a woman to woo a man, for it is the loser
who seeks what he lost [the rib].

TALMUD

*The only true love is love at first sight: second
sight dispels it.*

ISRAEL ZANGWILL

The Holy One, blessed be He, gave greater
understanding to women than to men.

TALMUD

A rich man's daughter is always a beauty.

SAYING

A man who takes a wife for the sake of money will have unworthy children.

TALMUD

'I want you to meet my boyfriend, Gerry,' said Amanda to her parents, Mr and Mrs Cohen.

'So, what do you do for a living?' asked Mr Cohen.

'I own some property,' replied Gerry.

'Some property!' cried Amanda. 'Gerry owns practically all of the Docklands.'

'And where do you live?' asked Mrs Cohen.

'Um . . . in the Finchley area,' answered the young man.

'Finchley!' exclaimed Amada. 'Gerry lives in a mansion in The Bishop's Avenue, no less.'

'And your prospects?' asked Mr Cohen.

'I'm hoping to expand.'

'*Expand!*' interrupted Amanda. 'Gerry's about to buy Brent Cross Shopping Centre.'

At that point Gerry sneezed.

'You got a cold?' asked Mrs Cohen.

'A cold?' gasped Amanda. 'Gerry's got pneumonia!'

I am a rose of Sharon,
A lily of the valleys.
Like a lily among thorns,
So is my darling among the maidens.
Like an apple tree among trees of the forest,
So is my beloved among the youths.
I delight to sit in his shade,
And his fruit is sweet to my mouth . . .

My beloved spoke thus to me:
'Arise my darling;
My fair one, come away!
For now the winter is past,
The rains are over and gone,
The blossoms have appeared in the land,
The time of pruning has come;
The song of the turtledove
Is heard in our land.
The green figs form on the figtree,
The vines in blossom give off fragrance,
Arise, my darling;
My fair one, come away!'

How sweet is your love,
My own, my bride!
How much more delightful your love than
wine,
Your ointments more fragrant
Than any spice!
Sweetness drops
From your lips, O bride;
Honey and milk
Are under your tongue;
And the scent of your robes
Is like the scent of Lebanon . . .

Let me be a seal upon your heart,
Like the seal upon your hand.
For love is fierce as death,
Passion is mighty as Sheol;
Its darts are darts of fire,
A blazing flame.
Vast floods cannot quench love,
Nor rivers drown it.
If a man offered all his wealth for love,
He would be laughed to scorn.

SONG OF SONGS

I've never loved a man I liked, and never liked a man I loved.

FANNY BRICE

Where there is love one can sleep on the edge of a sword,
Where there is none, a bed of sixty cubits is insufficient.

TALMUD

Caught kissing a chorus girl by his wife,
Chico Marx declared, 'I wasn't kissing her.
I was whispering in her mouth.'

RSVP – Remember to Send Vedding
Presents.

Whoever called it necking was a poor judge
of anatomy.

GROUCHO MARX

David Freeman was going home on the train and was sitting next to a nice-looking young man.

'So,' asked David. 'Have you travelled far?'

'Well, yes actually,' replied the youth. 'I live in Edgware.'

'So what brings you to Rickmansworth?'

'I'm going to see someone.'

'Business?'

'No.'

'Are you married?'

'No.'

'I'm David Freeman.'

'Pleased to meet you. I'm Joshua Greenberg.'

'Aha!' David closed his eyes and started to piece things together. 'So,' he thought, 'he's schlepped all the way to Rickmansworth, looking smart and smelling of expensive aftershave. He's not coming here on business . . . so . . . he must be visiting a girl. Now he seems a polite young man, so he's not likely to be going behind his parents' back seeing a non-Jewish girl. There aren't many nice and single Jewish girls left in Rickmansworth. What about Joanna Bloom? No – she's just got engaged. Now about Gerry and Debbie's girl, Shelley? No – he's too clean cut for her. I suppose he could be seeing Rebecca Levin, but she's away on holiday. And Helen Goldblatt . . . no, she's not interested in men. So, I suppose that just leaves Suzanna Bernstein. She's a lovely girl, polite, pretty, about his age. Yes, that's why he's here.'

'Young man,' said David.'Let me be the

first to congratulate you on your forthcoming engagement to Suzanna Bernstein.'

'What? Mr Freeman! How did you know? Neither of us has told anyone yet. So how on earth . . . ?'

'My boy,' said David. 'It's absolutely obvious!'

———————⚘———————

One evening at an expensive New York restaurant, a young man, Bernie Rosenberg, approached Frank Sinatra and asked him for a favour.

'I'm here with a girl and I want to make a good impression on her. I certainly would appreciate it if you would drop by my table and say "Hi Berni!" '

'Sure, kid, I'll try,' laughed Sinatra.

As he was about to leave, Sinatra went over to Bernie's table and said, 'Hi there, Bernie!'

'Don't bother me now, Frankie,' snapped Rosenberg. 'Can't you see I'm busy!'

A woman of valour who can find?
For her price is far above rubies.
The heart of her husband does safely trust
in her,
And he has no lack of gain.
She does him good and not evil
All the days of her life.
She seeks wool and flax,
And works willingly with her hands.
She is like the merchant-ships;
She brings her food from afar.
She rises also while it is still night,
And gives food to her household,
And a portion to her maidens.
She considers a field and buys it;
With the fruit of her hands she plants a
vineyard.
She girds her loins with strength.
And makes strong her arms.
She perceives that her merchandise is
good;
Her lamp goes not out by night.
She lays her hand to the distaff,
And her hands hold the spindle.
She stretches out her hand to the poor;
Yea, she reaches forth her hand to the
needy.

She is not afraid of the snow for her
household;
For all her household are clothed in scarlet.
She makes for herself coverlets;
Her clothing is fine linen and purple.
Her husband is known in the gates,
When he sits among the elders of the land.
She makes linen garments and sells them;
And delivers girdles unto the merchant.
Strength and dignity are her clothing;
And she laughs at the time to come.
She opens her mouth with wisdom;
And the law of kindness is on her tongue.
She looks well to the ways of her
household.
And eats not the bread of idleness.
Her children rise up and call her blessed;
Her husband also, and he praises her:
Many daughters have done valiantly,
But you exceed them all.
Grace is deceitful, and beauty is vain;
But a woman that fears the Lord, she shall
be praised.
Give her of the fruit of her hands;
and let her works praise her in the gates.

PROVERBS, Ch 31, v 10–31

A man who could not marry off his ugly daughter visited Rabbi Shimonel of Cracow. 'My heart is heavy,' he told the Rabbi, 'because the Lord has given me an ugly daughter.'

'How ugly?' the Seer asked.

'If she were lying on a plate with a herring you wouldn't be able to tell the difference.'

The Seer of Cracow thought for a while and finally asked, 'What kind of herring?'

The man, taken aback by the query, thought quickly and said, 'Er – Bismarck.'

'Too bad,' said the Rabbi. 'If it was Maatjes, she'd have a better chance.'

WOODY ALLEN

I don't know much about classical music. For years I thought the 'Goldberg Variations' were something Mr and Mrs Goldberg tried on their wedding night.

WOODY ALLEN

On my wedding night my wife stopped in the middle of everything to give me a standing ovation.

WOODY ALLEN

I didn't marry the first girl I fell in love with . . . because there was a tremendous religious conflict at the time. She was an atheist and I was an agnostic. We didn't know what religion *not* to bring the children up in.

WOODY ALLEN

It was the day that the nuns were being inducted into the Order. Just before the ceremony started two old Jewish women entered the Catholic Church and sat down in the front pew.

One of the older Sisters went up to the old women. 'Hello, ladies. As you can see, we have an important ceremony about to occur here. . .'

'Don't worry,' interrupted one of the old Jewish women. 'We're from the groom's side!'

It is easier for an apathetic man to be stirred to enjoyment than for a man burning with passion to curb his lusts.

MAIMONIDES

It was the custom in ancient Judea that a cedar tree was planted when a boy was born and an acacia tree when a girl was born. When they grew up and married, their wedding canopy was made of branches woven from both trees.

TALMUD

Everyone knows why a bride enters the bridal chamber... But if someone makes obscene comments about it, even if that person was destined for seventy years of happiness, the decree is changed to one of unhappiness.

TALMUD

The duty of regular sexual intercourse is, according to the Torah:

 people who do not need to work for a living
 – every day;
 labourers – twice a week;
 ass-drivers – once a week;
 camel-drivers – once every thirty days;
 sailors – once every six months.

Harry Goldblum told his three children that he had an important announcement to make. So all three assembled in his house to hear their father's news.

'Children,' said Harry. 'As you know I have been very lonely since your mother passed away ten years ago and now, at the age of seventy, I've decided to give myself a little happiness. So, I'm going to remarry . . . a lovely, sweet girl, a wonderful cook, a marvellous housekeeper . . .'

'Girl?' echoed his daughter Louise. 'Did you say *girl*?'

'And how old is this *girl*?' asked David, his son.

'Twenty years old.'

'*Twenty years old*!' shrieked Janice, the third child. 'How can you even think of such a thing?'

'Children, children,' cried Harry. 'What's your problem? After all, when I married your mother she wasn't even nineteen!'

Our Rabbis taught: If the woman has her orgasm first, she will bear a male, and if the man has his orgasm first, she will bear a female. Therefore those who restrain themselves in intercourse to enable their wives to have their orgasm first acquire great merit.

Rava said, 'Anyone who wants all his children to be males should have intercourse twice in succession.'

TALMUD

Our passions are like travellers: at first they make a brief stay; then they are like guests, who visit often; and then they turn into tyrants, who hold us in their power.

TALMUD

A man once developed an overwhelming longing for a certain woman, and he became sick with desire for her.

The doctors consulted declared, 'He will be cured only if she submits.'

But the sages said, 'Let him die rather than have her submit.'

The doctors then said, 'Let her stand nude before him.'

To which the sages answered, 'Sooner let him die.'

'Then,' said the doctors, 'let her speak with him from behind a fence.'

'Let him die,' the sages maintained, 'rather than even have her speak with him from behind a fence.'

Why not have the man marry her?

Marriage would not satisfy his passion, even as Rabbi Isaac said: since the destruction of the Temple, sexual pleasure has been taken away from those who practise it lawfully and given to sinners, as it is written, 'Stolen waters are sweet, and bread eaten in secret is pleasant'.

TALMUD

An Israeli fisherman has been standing patiently on the beach for hours with his fishing rod. All he's caught so far are two meagre sardines. Suddenly there's a tug on the line and there's no doubt he's hooked a big one.

As he begins to reel in his line, a giant fish comes out of the water and says, 'Put me back, put me back in the sea and I'll fulfil any wish you make.'

'Really? Anything?' The fisherman takes a map out of his pocket and spreads it out before the fish.

'Here's little, tiny Israel surrounded by Egypt, which has oil, Saudi Arabia, which has plenty of oil, all the Emirates have lots of oil, Iraq has oil, Iran has oil, Syria has oil. All I'm asking you is why not put a few oil wells near Eilat, a few round Beersheba, a few around Tel Aviv, a few round Haifa and in Galilee . . .'

'Hold on, hold on,' says the fish, 'that's a very complicated geopolitical issue involving OPEC, the big oil companies, the various governments, borders . . . You don't want to become embroiled in all that. Ask me for something a bit simpler, something more personal.'

'Okay,' says the fisherman. 'I've been married ten years to this beautiful Jewish princess and she won't let me make love to her more than once a month. Ah, please, why not once a week or, better still, three times a week?'

'Hold on, hold on,' says the fish, 'let's see that map again . . .'

Father Stack called Rabbi Blumberg in a state of panic.

'Rabbi,' cried the priest,'I've got a problem and no other priest is available to help me. You're a good friend, help me out please!'

'Sure, I'll help,' replied the rabbi. 'What's the problem?'

'Come over to my church and I'll tell you.'

When Rabbi Blumberg arrived at the church, Father Stack told him what the problem was. 'I'm supposed to be taking a funeral in a half an hour, but I've got confessions starting in fifteen minutes. Can you take the confessions for me?'

'Sure, but what am I supposed to do?'

'Just listen to me for a few minutes and then take over. Honestly there's nothing to it!'

The rabbi sat near the confessional box so he could hear the priest and shortly afterwards a woman entered:

'Father, Father, I have sinned. I need forgiveness.'

'What have you done, my child?'

'I have committed adultery, Father.'

'How many times?'

'Six times, Father,' wept the woman.

'Say six Hail Marys and put three pounds in the offertory box. Then, my child, you will be absolved.'

Then another woman entered. She too had committed adultery: she'd made love to her boss four times.

'Say four Hail Marys and put two pounds in the box. Then you will be absolved.'

At this point the priest had to leave and

whispered to the rabbi, 'You see, it's easy. I'm sure you'll have no problems!'

The rabbi went in to the confessional and moments later another woman entered.

'Father, Father, I have sinned terribly. I have committed adultery.'

'How many times, my child?' asked Rabbi Blumberg.

'Only once, Father,' whispered the woman.

'Well, I think you'd better do it once more!'

'What? Commit adultery *again*? !'

'Absolutely,' replied the rabbi, 'it's two for a pound.'

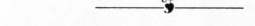

A man is young if a lady can make him happy or unhappy.

He enters middle age if a lady can make him happy, but can no longer make him unhappy.

He is old and gone if a lady can make him neither happy nor unhappy.

MORITZ ROSENTHAL

What's the definition of a Jewish nymphomaniac?
Someone who will make love on the same day she's had her hair done.

MAUREEN LIPMAN

What's the definition of Jewish foreplay?
Three hours of begging.

MAUREEN LIPMAN

How do you know that a Jewish woman has had an orgasm?
She drops her nail file.

'David,' moaned Harold, 'my wife's become a real sex object!'
  'So, why are you complaining?' asked David.
  'Because, every time I suggest sex, she objects!'

Heidi Abromowitz – the girl was a tramp from the moment her mother's waters broke. You think I'm kidding? When the doctor spanked her at birth, she cried out for more!

JOAN RIVERS

If he was young and she old or if he was old and she young, he is told, 'What would you with a young woman?' or 'What would you with an old woman? Go to one who is of the same age as yourself and create no strife in your home!'

TALMUD

The other night I said to my wife Ruth, 'Do you feel that the sex and excitement has gone out of our marriage?' Ruth said, 'I'll discuss it with you during the next commercial.'

MILTON BERLE

In sex and in love human character is revealed more than anywhere else.

Let's say a man tries to play a very strong man: a big man, a dictator. But in sex he may become reduced to a child or to an imp. The sexual organs are the most sensitive organs of the human being. The eye or the ear seldom sabotage you. An eye cannot stop seeing if it doesn't like what it sees, but the penis will stop functioning if he doesn't like what he sees. I would say that the sexual organs express the human soul more than any other part of the body. They are not diplomats. They tell the truth ruthlessly . . . They are even more *meshuga* than the brain.

ISAAC BASHEVIS SINGER

After the preview of a Doris Day film, Groucho Marx was asked if he knew Doris Day.

'Shucks,' exclaimed Marx, 'I knew her before she was a virgin.'

A man's only as old as the woman he feels.

GROUCHO MARX

When he was accused of being obsessed with sex, Groucho Marx argued, 'It's not an obsession, it's a talent.'

Give me my golf clubs, fresh air and a beautiful partner, and you can keep my golf clubs and the fresh air.

JACK BENNY

What does an Italian woman say when she's making love?
'Ooh! Ahhh! Che Meravigliosa!'
An English woman?
'Gosh! You do kiss jolly well!'
A Jewish woman?
'Morry! The ceiling needs painting!'

You should treat a cigar like a mistress; put it away before you are sick of it.

BENJAMIN DISRAELI

Were it not for the Evil Impulse, no man would build a house, marry a wife, or beget children.

GENESIS RABBAH

*M*arriage is like a warm bath. Once you get used to it, it's not so hot.

JOEY ADAMS

He who has no wife lives without joy, without blessing, and without good.

TALMUD

Student: Rabbi, could you tell me why the Lord made man before woman?
Rabbi: Because he didn't want advice on how to create man!

'Why does a bride wear white on her wedding day?' asked the teacher.

No one answered.

'Well, white stands for joy and the wedding day is the most joyous occasion of a woman's life.'

'Sir?' asked little Danny. 'So, why do all the men wear black?'

A man should always be careful not to wrong his wife, for since she cries easily, she is quickly hurt . . .

A man must be careful about the respect with which he treats his wife, because blessings rest on his home only on account of her.

And this is what Rava said to the townspeople of Mahoza: Honour your wives so that you may be enriched.

TALMUD

'Sweetheart! Sweetheart! Your honeybunny's home. Where are you?'

'I'm hiding.'

'Sweetheart, I've got a surprise for you. Where are you?'

'I'm hiding.'

'I bought you those diamond earrings you wanted from the jeweller's. Where are you?'

'I'm hiding . . . behind the sofa in the living room.'

A seventy-year-old man goes into a Catholic church and enters the confessional.

'Father,' says the old man, 'I am seventy years old and last week I spent the afternoon with a twenty-two-year-old girl. She was the most wonderful woman I've ever met and we made love three times. It's never happened to me, Simon Leibowitz, before in my life.'

The priest stopped him. 'Simon Leibowitz – are you a member of my congregation?'

'No, Father. I belong to the synagogue across the road.'

'So why don't you go and tell all this to your rabbi, Simon?'

'Oh, I've already told him – I want everybody to know.'

A man rejoices when he dwells in his own home.

TALMUD

Very late one night, Samuel Goldwyn
decided to phone Arthur Loew in New York,
unaware of the time differences.

When he picked up the phone, Loew yelled
at Goldwyn: 'Sam! Do you have any idea
what time it is? !'

'Frances,' said Goldwyn to his wife,
'Arthur wants to know what the time is.'

Two Jewish men were discussing their
wives.

'My wife drives me crazy,' declared David,
'every night she dreams she's married to a
millionaire!'

'That drives you crazy? You're lucky! My
wife dreams she's married to a millionaire
during the daytime!'

A good wife makes a happy husband; she doubles the length of his life.

A staunch wife is her husband's joy; he will live out his days in peace.

A good wife means a good life; she is one of the Lord's gifts to those who fear Him . . .

A wife's charm is the delight of her husband, and her womanly skill puts flesh on his bones . . .

As bright as the light on the sacred lampstand is a beautiful face in the settled prime of life.

Like a golden pillar on a silver base is a shapely leg with a firm foot.

WISDOM OF BEN SIRA

I love being married . . . It's so great to find that one special person you want to annoy for the rest of your life.

RITA RUDNER

I hate housework! You make the beds, you do the dishes – and six months later you have to start all over again!

JOAN RIVERS

Neville Goldblum went to Selfridges. 'I want to buy a really nice fountain pen for my wife. It's her birthday next week.'

'Ah, that will be a nice surprise for her, I'm sure,' said the sales assistant.

'It certainly will be,' said Mr Goldblum. 'She's expecting a fur coat!'

Warren had just received the phone bill. He called his wife and children in to the kitchen.

'Now listen, eight hundred pounds is a ridiculous sum for the quarter. Seeing as I never use this phone, I want you all to promise to cut down on your calls.'

'Yes, yes, yes,' replied his family,

For a couple of days, Warren was pleased to see that they were taking notice of him. A week later however, even Warren conceded the family could never really cooperate. One night he came home to find his wife dialling a number. A quarter of an hour later she put the receiver down.

'Wow!' he exclaimed. 'That was short. How come you were on the phone only for a quarter of an hour?'

'It was a wrong number, darling!'

Harry and Maureen, on holiday in Marbella, were watching a grand procession before the bull fight, and Maureen was asking her husband endless questions.

'Who's that leading the procession?'

'The toreador,' answered Harry.

'And behind him?' asked Maureen.

'The matador.'

'And behind him?'

'The picador.'

'And who's that little man behind him?'

'That's Isadore, the kosher butcher.'

A mistress is what goes between a mister and a mattress.

JOE E LEWIS

G-d did not create woman from man's head that he should command her.

nor from his feet
that she should be his slave,

but rather from his side
that she should
be near his heart.

TALMUD

Shelley and Morry are in bed and Shelley is having trouble sleeping. She says to her husband, 'Morry, turn over.'

'£45,765,' he replied . . .

'My wife is so well read,' said Shapiro. 'She goes to evening classes, lectures and is so up-to-date with current affairs that she can talk all night on any subject.'

'My wife,' boasted Steinberg, 'doesn't *need* a subject.'

One stormy night, Monty Bloom, soaked to the skin, ran into the delicatessen.

'A smoked salmon bagel and a salt beef sandwich please,' said Monty to the man behind the counter. 'Oh, and some of your strudel, cheesecake and lockshen pudding.'

'Is that all?' asked the assistant.

'Yes, I think that's all she wanted,' said Monty, his teeth chattering.

'For your wife is it?'

'My wife? Of course it's for my wife! You think my *mother* would send me out on a night like this?'

This is the work that a wife should do for her husband: grinding flour, baking bread, washing clothes, cooking food, suckling her child, making his bed, and working in wool.

If, however, she brought into the marriage one bondwoman, she need not grind or bake or wash.

If she brought in two bondwomen, she need not cook or suckle her child.

If she brought in three bondwomen, she need not make his bed or work in wool.

If she brought in four bondwomen, she may sit in a chair all day.

MISHNAH

'Women reach their sexual peak at thirty-five, but men at 18. The Lord must believe in practical jokes: we reach our sexual peak when they're discovering their favourite chair!'

RITA RUDNER

Hence a man leaves his father and mother and clings to his wife, so that they become one flesh.

GENESIS

Rabbi Johanan said: If a man's first wife dies, it is as if the Temple were destroyed in his day.
Rabbi Alexandri said: If a man's wife dies, the world becomes dark for him.
Rabbi Samuel ben Nahman said: For everything there is a substitute except for the wife of one's youth.
Rabbi Akiba said: He is wealthy who has a virtuous wife.

TALMUD

A Jewish wife is unwell, sick, ill, very ill, very very sick, terribly ill, dangerously sick, a widow.

'Help me Rabbi!' cried the man. 'I have a wife and nine children. I cannot support them. Every year my wife gives me a new child. What shall I do?'

'Do?' answered the rabbi. 'Take my advice and do absolutely nothing!'

Hymie and Ruth were celebrating their wedding anniversary and Hymie decided to buy his wife a string of pearls. So, he went to the jeweller's and asked to see the selection of pearl necklaces

'This one, sir,' said the assistant, 'is our best necklace. The pearls are one hundred per cent cultured!'

'Cultured, schmultured, who cares? I just want to buy my Ruthie simple pearls. Let someone else pay for their university degree!'

Happy is the man with a wife to tell him what to do, and a secretary to do it.

LORD MANCROFT

On their thirtieth wedding anniversary, Renee turned to her husband Jack:
  'Will you still love me when my hair has turned to grey?'
  'Why not?' he replied. 'Haven't I loved you through five other shades?'

There was once a pious man who was married to a pious woman, and they did not have any children.

They said, 'We are of no use to G-d,' and they divorced one another.

The man went and married a wicked woman, and she made him wicked.

The woman went and married a wicked man, and she made him good.

This proves that all depends on the woman.

GENESIS RABBAH

Chico: I would like to say goodbye to your wife.
Groucho: Who wouldn't?

Groucho: So how many children do you have, madam?
Contestant: I have thirteen.
Groucho: Thirteen? !
Contestant: I love my husband.
Groucho: I love my cigar but I still take it out once in a while.

I bought my wife a new car. She called me and said there was water in the carburettor. I said where's the car? She said in the lake.

HENNY YOUNGMAN

Marriage is like a violin. When the beautiful music is over, the strings are still attached.

When Adam came home late one night,
   what was the first thing Eve did?
She counted his ribs.

If you're going to do something wrong, at least enjoy it.

SAYING

Show me a Jewish man who comes home early every night, is greeted with smiles and coos, has his coat and hat taken, his shoes taken off, pillows arranged for him, made to feel comfortable and welcome in every way, then is served a really delicious meal – and I'll show you a Jew who lives in a Japanese restaurant.

JOE E LEWIS

Morry: Hello Sam, how's your wife?
Sam: Compared to whom?

Zsa Zsa Gabor is an expert housekeeper. Every time she gets divorced, she keeps the house.

HENNY YOUNGMAN

'Did you see Leonard's fiancée?' cried Fay. 'What a bimbo! 38–24–34, such a bosom! And that hair, so dyed! And her clothes – tight leather mini-skirt and such a skimpy see-through blouse! Believe me, Harry, that marriage won't last a year.'

'I should have such a year!' sighed Harry.

'Ruth, I don't understand you,' remarked her friend Esther.

'Why's that?' asked Ruth.

'Well, I don't understand how you can be so good-natured about your Jack.'

'Jack?'

'Yes,' replied Esther. 'You never seem to mind him running after young dollybirds.'

'Esther, Esther,' laughed Ruth. 'A dog runs after motor cars, but when it catches up with one, can it drive it?'

———————

The Rabbi started his Shabbat sermon: 'Today, I feel that I must discuss the breaking of the commandments. It seems to me that there are various members of this congregation who indulge in . . . adultery.'

There was a hush in the synagogue. Suddenly Harry Cohen, who had been dozing, woke up with a start. 'That's it!' he cried. 'That's where I must have lost my wallet!'

———————

'Shirley, how can you tell if Harry's lying to you?' asked Maureen.

'By looking at his face,' replied Shirley.

'Just by looking at his face?' repeated Maureen.

'Sure. If his lips are moving . . . he's lying!'

There were two queues in Heaven, one for men who dominated their wives, the other for men who'd been dominated by their wives. The latter queue wound right round the blocks of Heaven. The former queue only had one man in it. St Peter opened the gate and said 'Gosh, it's a long time since we've had anyone standing in the queue for men who dominated their wives. What are you doing here?' The man replied: 'My wife told me to stand here.'

MAUREEN LIPMAN

Two Jewish women meet outside the hairdresser's.

'What a wonderful hairstyle,' cried Ruth. 'You're looking so well, so *youthful*.'

'You want to know my secret?' asked Renee.

'Of course I do, Renee!'

'Between you and me, Ruthie, I'm having an affair!'

'An affair! That's marvellous! So, tell me, who are the caterers?'

As Danny and David undressed before their workout, Danny watched incredulously as David started to unhook his corset.

'Wow, David,' exclaimed Danny. 'Since when have you been wearing a corset?'

'Since my wife found it in the glove compartment!'

———————✣———————

Mrs Cohen: So, did you enjoy dinner, darling?

Mr Cohen: It was lovely, sweetheart. Did you see that woman who walked past our table before – the one in the green dress?

Mrs Cohen: Did I see the woman in the green dress? You couldn't fail to notice her. She should wear such a shade with her colouring? And did you see the way the dress hung? I wouldn't inflict such hanging on curtains.

Mr Cohen: Still, she had a beautiful face.

Mrs Cohen: Well, at least it distracts from that corset she was wearing. But that blue eyeshadow – in the 1970s she would have been fashionable. And those thin lips – 'luscious pink' somehow clashes with those black roots underneath the peroxide.

Mr Cohen: Well, the overall effect was quite stunning.

Mrs Cohen: I couldn't say for sure. I didn't take a good look at her.

I've been in love with the same woman for forty-one years. If my wife finds out, she'll kill me.

HENNY YOUNGMAN

Deborah and Helena were shopping and filling each other in on their gossip.

'I must tell you what's happened,' said Helena. 'On Monday morning a gorgeous young man came to the door and asked for Melvyn. When I said he'd left for work, the man picked me up, took me upstairs and made mad, passionate love to me. On Tuesday at about midday, he came to the house again and asked "Where's Melvyn?" "At the office," I told him, and he then proceeded to undress me on the stairs. It was fantastic, Deborah . . . the same thing happened on Wednesday and Thursday – the same question followed by steamy sex. I never knew it could be so wonderful. But one thing worries me.'

'What?' asked Deborah, green with envy.

'What on *earth* does he want with Melvyn?'

My grandmother buried three husbands – two of them were just napping.

RITA RUDNER

'**I**'m absolutely sick of Judy,' said Jack to his friend David. 'She's always moaning. Whatever I give her, she complains. Last month I bought her perfume, gold earrings, a new dishwasher, a brand new bathroom suite and only yesterday I came home with a Golf convertible which she didn't want. She is *never* satisfied.'

'That's it!' replied David. 'The Golf! Get her a Jaguar instead.'

A few days later, David and Jack met at the bridge club.

'David, David!' cried Jack. 'You're fantastic! It worked!'

'What worked, Jack?' asked David.

'The Jaguar. One bite and she was dead. No more moaning now!'

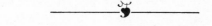

'**H**ave I had a bad month,' cried Sarah to her friend Rebecca.

'So I've heard,' replied Rebecca. 'Is it true that your Harry ran off with his secretary?'

'Yes, and that's not all!' moaned Sarah. 'The business has gone bust, my seventeen-year-old daughter's become pregnant, Sheldon dropped out of law school to become an actor and now – you'll never guess . . .'

'What?' gasped Rebecca.

'. . . I've got the decorators in!'

'Rabbi,' complained Morry. 'I've been told that Renée is sorry she divorced me. What shall I do?'

'Absolutely nothing,' replied the Rabbi.

'Really?' asked Morry, slightly surprised.

'Yes, Morry. You have to understand something . . . wives are like fishermen: they complain about the one they've caught and brag about the one that got away!'

Mrs Bernstein went to her local police station to report the disappearance of her husband.

'My husband has gone missing! Please find him for me – I can't live without him' exclaimed Mrs Bernstein.

'Right, madam,' replied the desk sergeant. 'Can you describe him for me? Then we can put out a search for him.'

'Well, he's fifty-five, balding, with a big belly. He sweats a lot and he's got very thick glasses, because he's short-sighted and . . . hang on, sergeant, on second thoughts maybe you shouldn't bother . . .'

Music played at weddings always reminds me of the music played for soldiers before they go off to battle.

HEINRICH HEINE

On his deathbed, Heinrich Heine insisted on changing his will. He added a new clause which left everything to his wife on the condition she remarried after his death. The reason?

'When Matilda remarries there will be at least one man who will regret my death.'

A henpecked Jewish husband was told by a messenger that his wife had been killed in a road accident. The man remained expressionless.

'Your wife has been killed, sir,' repeated the messenger, 'and you show no emotion, no emotion at all!'

'If you had toothache like I do,' said the man, 'you'd have trouble smiling, too!'

The following may be compelled to divorce their wives: A man who is afflicted with boils, or has a goitre, or gathers dog excrements [for use in tanning], or is a coppersmith or a tanner [whose work makes him smell bad], whether these conditions existed before they married or arose after marriage.

Above all these, Rabbi Meir said: 'Although the husband may have made an agreement with her that she marry him in spite of these defects, she may plead, "I thought I could endure him, but I cannot".'

MISHNAH

When a divorced man marries a divorced woman, there are four minds in one bed.

SAYING

Alimony: the bounty after the mutiny.

MAX KAUFFMANN

In Hollywood, marriage is a success if it outlives milk.

RITA RUDNER

The Grand Rabbi didn't raise his eyes from his books when he asked the woman crying opposite him what her complaint was.

She told him that her husband had been gone for three months and there was no sign he was ever coming home. He had left her with four small children and there was no one to provide for them.

The Rabbi asked her name, her husband's name, her mother's name, his mother's name, etc, etc, turned the pages of the books back and forth, and finally, slapping his hand firmly on the table, said, with his eyes closed as in a trance, 'Woman, go home. There is no doubt your husband will return within the coming four weeks.'

As the woman was leaving the Rabbi's room, the Shamash (his assistant) whispered in her ear, 'Woman, forget it. Your husband will not return.'

Five weeks later the woman was once more sobbing in front of the Rabbi's desk whilst he went again through her name, her husband's name, her mother's name, his mother's name, etc, etc, all the while checking through the pages of another book and another book and another book. Finally, very finally, he slapped the pile of books before him and, gazing at his desk, declared, 'Woman, go home. In two weeks' time your husband will return. No doubt about it – I can see it in the books.'

As the woman was happily leaving the Rabbi's room, again the Shamash whispered in her ear, 'Forget it, woman. Your husband is not coming back.'

After the woman had gone, the Rabbi summoned the Shamash to his desk and said, 'Do you think that I haven't heard you whispering to the woman? I heard it the first time as well. How dare you contradict me?'

To this the Shamash replied, 'Dear Rabbi, the difference between you and me is that you are looking in the books while I look at her face. Her husband will not return to her.'

A very old Jewish couple went to a divorce lawyer. 'We want a divorce,' they declared.

The lawyer looked at them. 'You're both over ninety years old. Are you sure you want to divorce?'

'Yes,' they answered. 'We've been married for over seventy years and we have never really got on well together.'

'So, why have you waited so long?' asked the bemused lawyer.

'We didn't want to upset the children, so we waited for them to die!'

Two women meet on the street.

'Miriam, I hear congratulations are in order!'

'Yes, my Ruthie's getting married.'

'Mazeltov! and who's the lucky man?'

'David – a solicitor in one of the top firms in the country, no less.'

'Fantastic! But you know, Miriam, for some reason I thought he was an academic.'

'Ah, you're thinking of her first husband, Gerry, the University Professor.'

'Yes, I remember. Didn't he teach medicine or biology?'

'No, no, no, that was Simon, the plastic surgeon and gynaecologist. He was her second husband.'

'Oh Miriam, you're such a lucky woman. So much naches from just one child!'

We pondered whether to take a vacation or get a divorce and decided that a trip to Bermuda is over in two weeks, but a divorce is something you always have.

WOODY ALLEN

The Horowitzs' divorce case had come before the judge.

'Mrs Horowitz,' asked the judge. 'How old are you?'

'Thirty years old,' replied the grey-haired Mrs Horowitz.

'Please answer the question truthfully,' said the judge.

'I'm thirty years old,' repeated the woman.

'Well, I have your birth certificate in front of me,' said the judge, 'and according to this you were born in 1942. That makes you over fifty.'

'Your honour,' interrupted Mrs Horowitz. 'I'm not including the last twenty years with my husband, of course.'

'Why not?'

'You call that *living*?'

_____

Jack and Harry were walking around the golf course.

'I want a divorce,' said Jack, all of a sudden.

'What?' cried Harry. 'You want to divorce Michelle? But she's so lovely. She's soft and gentle and not only that, she's *beautiful*. She's still got a good figure, really well proportioned . . .'

Jack took off his golf shoe. 'Take a good look at this shoe,' he said. 'The leather is soft and gentle. It's a beautiful shoe to look at and many would say it's nicely proportioned.'

'I still don't understand,' said Harry.

'Well, Harry, it's like this, I'm the only one who knows . . . that it pinches like hell!'

My idea of an agreeable person
is a person who agrees with
me.

BENJAMIN DISRAELI

There are four types of temperament:
Easy to provoke and easy to calm. Here the fault is cancelled by the virtue.
Hard to provoke, but hard to calm. Here the virtue is cancelled by the fault.
Hard to provoke, and easy to calm. This is the temperament of a good man.
Easy to provoke, but hard to calm. This is the temperament of a wicked man.

TALMUD

The best part about telling the truth is that you don't have to remember what you said.

SAYING

Why is gossip like a three-pronged tongue? Because it kills three people: the person who says it, the person who listens to it, and the person about whom it is said.

TALMUD

*L*ike a great poet, Nature is capable of
producing the most stunning effects with the
smallest means. Nature possesses only the
sun, trees, flowers, water and love. But for
him who feels no love in his heart, none of
these things has any poetic value. To such an
individual the sun has a diameter of a certain
number of miles, the trees are good for
making a fire, the flowers are divided into
varieties, and water is wet.

HEINRICH HEINE

*H*e who in his life has never made a fool of
himself has also never been wise.

HEINRICH HEINE

A stingy person and a fat cow are useful only *after they are dead.*

SHOLOM ALEICHEM

Was *pretty,* had *money,* could *sing – all these are absolutely useless.*

SHOLOM ALEICHEM

A little sincerity is a dangerous thing, and a great deal of it is absolutely fatal.

BENJAMIN DISRAELI

A quarrel is like an itch: the more you scratch, the more it itches.

SAYING

Better an insincere peace than a sincere quarrel.

THE LUBLINER RABBI

Rejoice not when your enemy falls,
   And let not your heart be glad when he
stumbles . . .
If your enemy is hungry, give him bread to
eat,
   And if he is thirsty, give him water to drink.

PROVERBS

A sin committed with good intentions is better than a good deed performed for the wrong motives.

TALMUD

*B*enjamin *Disraeli's way of pleasing Queen Victoria:*
  'I never deny; I never contradict; I sometimes forget.'

*T*he space in a needle's eye is sufficient for two friends, but the whole world is scarcely big enough to hold two enemies.

IBN GABRIOL

At first the Evil Impulse is as fragile as the thread of a spider, but eventually it becomes as tough as cart ropes.

TALMUD

If I am not for myself, who is for me?
And if I am only for myself, what am I?
And if not now, when?

ETHICS OF THE FATHERS

There are three types of man whose life is not worth living: he who must eat at another's table, he whose wife rules over him, and he whose body is racked by pain.

TALMUD

Think of Disraeli, *for whom any Jewish community would have been too confining since the British Empire was hardly big enough for him.*

MAX NORDAU

It is easier to fight for principles than to live up to them.

ALFRED ADLER

For the sake of peace one may lie, but peace itself should never be a lie.

SAYING

One is a lie, two are lies, but three lies becomes politics.

SAYING

If Presidents don't do it to their wives, they do it to the country.

MEL BROOKS

Those who have nothing are always eager to share it with others.

SAYING

We have to believe in free will. We've got no choice.

ISAAC BASHEVIS SINGER

Rabban Simeon ben Gamaliel had said: 'The world rests on three things: on justice, on truth, on peace.' Said Rabbi Mona: 'But these three are one and the same: for if there is justice there is truth, and if there is truth, there is peace.'

TALMUD

My Philosophy of Life? Life is very simple. The first thing to remember about life is – don't worry about it. Really, there are only two things to worry about: either you're successful or you're not successful. If you're successful there's nothing to worry about. If you're not successful there's only two things to worry about: if your health is good there's nothing to worry about. If your health is bad there's only two things to worry about. Either you're going to live or you're not going to live. If you live there's nothing to worry about, and if you don't live, why you've only two things to worry about: either you're going to heaven or you're not going to heaven. If you go to heaven there's nothing to worry about, and if you go to the other place, you'll be so busy shaking hands with all your friends, *you won't have time to worry.*

MILTON BERLE

119

A season is set for everything, a time for
every experience under heaven.
A time for being born, and a time for dying.
A time for planting and a time for uprooting
the planted;
A time for slaying and a time for healing,
A time for tearing down and a time for
building up;
A time for weeping and a time for laughing,
A time for wailing and a time for dancing;
A time for throwing stones and a time for
gathering stones,
A time for embracing and a time for
shunning embraces;
A time for seeking and a time for losing,
A time for keeping and a time for
discarding;
A time for ripping and a time for sewing,
A time for silence and a time for speaking;
A time for loving and a time for hating;
A time for war and a time for peace.

ECCLESIASTES 3:1–8

Clever people are like fragrant roses: when you smell one rose, it's delightful, but smelling a whole bouquet may give you a headache.

MORITZ SAPHIR

The virtue of angels is that they cannot deteriorate; their flaw is that they cannot improve. Man's flaw is that he can deteriorate; and his virtue is that he can improve.

SAYING

When I see no way of teaching a truth except by pleasing one intelligent man and offending ten thousand fools, I address myself to the one, and ignore the censure of the multitude.

MAIMONIDES

A wise man is better than a strong man,
And a man of knowledge than a man of might;
For by wise guidance you wage war,
And victory lies in a wealth of counsellors.

PROVERBS

Carl Reiner recalls an incident in a New York restaurant, involving Mel Brooks:

'In 1959, I appeared in a movie called *Happy Anniversary*, and Mel came to the wrap party for the cast and crew at a restaurant in the Village. Moss Hart was dining with his wife on the other side of the room. Mel recognized him. All of a sudden he got up and walked across to Hart's table and said, very loudly, "Hello. You don't know who I am. My name is Mel Brooks. Do you know who you are? Your name is Moss Hart. Do you know what you've written? You wrote *Once in a Lifetime* with George Kaufman and *You Can't Take it With You* and *The Man Who Came to Dinner*. You wrote *Lady in the Dark* and you directed *My Fair Lady*." And he ran right through the list of Hart's credits. "You should be more arrogant!" he shouted. "You have earned the right to be supercilious! *Why* are you letting *me* talk to *you*?" '

Who is wise?
The man who can learn something from every man.

Who is strong?
The man who overcomes his passion.

Who is rich?
The man who is content with his fate.

Whom do men honour?
The man who honours his fellow men.

ETHICS OF THE FATHERS

A pseudo-scholar is like a donkey that carries a load of books.

THE ZOHAR

History is nothing but the soul's old wardrobe.

HEINRICH HEINE

———————⚡———————

Silence is restful: it gives rest to the heart, the larynx, the tongue, the lips, and the mouth.

THE ZOHAR

Good men need no monuments: their acts remain their shrines.

MISHNAH

*In 1934 there was great speculation that
Chaim Bialik, the Jewish Ukrainian poet, was
to receive the Nobel Prize for Literature. When
he failed to win the prize, Bialik admitted,
'I'm very glad I didn't win the prize. Now
everybody's my friend and feels sorry for me.
My, my how angry they are on my behalf.
"Now isn't that a scandal," they say.
"Imagine such a thing – Bialik, the great poet
Bialik, doesn't get the Nobel Prize! And just
look who they gave it to! To X, that so-and-
so! Why, he can't even hold a candle to
Bialik!"*

*'On the other hand,' he continued, 'what if
I had been awarded the Nobel Prize? Then
I'm sure some of the very same people who
are now so indignant on my account would
have said, "What's so wonderful about getting
the Nobel Prize? Why, even that poet Bialik
got one!" '*

*The wise man does not speak before him that
is greater than he in wisdom:*
he does not break into his fellow's speech;
he is not in a rush to reply;
*he asks what is relevant and replies to the
point;*
*he speaks of first things first and of last
things last;*
*of what he has not heard he says, 'I have
not heard,'*
and he acknowledges what is true;
And the opposites apply to the clod.

ETHICS OF THE FATHERS

*The aristrocracy is composed chiefly of asses
– asses who talk about horses.*

HEINRICH HEINE

He who forces time is forced back by time,
but he who yields to time finds time standing at his side.

TALMUD

'The point is that those who have been Divinely gifted in art, whether sculpture or painting and the like, have the privilege of being able to convert an inanimate thing, such as a brush, paint and canvas, or wood and stone, etc, into living form. In a deeper sense it is the ability to transform to a certain extent the material into spiritual, even where the creation is in still life, and certainly where the artistic work has to do with living creatures and humans. How much more so if the art medium is used to advance ideas, especially reflecting Torah and mitzvos, which would raise the artistic skill to its highest level.'

The Lubavitcher Rebbe, RABBI SCHNEERSON

Harpo was practising his harp one night in his hotel room when a neighbour knocked on the door, complaining, 'You play like King David, but not as well.'

'And you,' replied Harpo, 'speak like King Solomon, but not as wisely.'

On being introduced to Somerset Maugham, Harpo Marx confessed, 'I'm so glad to know you. I always thought Somerset Maugham was something like Epsom Downs or Stratford on Avon.'

When a man sits for an hour with a pretty girl on his knee it seems like a minute. But let him sit on a hot stove for a minute – and it's longer than an hour. That's relativity.

ALBERT EINSTEIN

When Albert Einstein was asked why he thought Germany, such an intellectual society, could succumb to the nonsense of Nazi ideology, he answered: 'The German people were imbued with three qualities: honesty, intelligence and Nazism. However, our Creator, in his wisdom, decreed that because we mortals are partly creatures of free will, a German could only possess two of the three qualities. That is why a German who is honest and also a Nazi cannot be intelligent. If he is intelligent and a Nazi, he cannot be honest. And if he is honest and intelligent, he cannot be a Nazi.'

A man should have no purpose in learning except this: to learn wisdom itself.

MAIMONIDES

Condemn no man
and consider nothing
impossible.

For there is no man who
does not have a future.

And there is nothing that
does not have
its hour.

TALMUD

*M*ost assuredly, you can say that Adam and Eve were communists. After all, they did not have a stitch of clothes on their bodies, had nothing to eat but apples, and they still thought they were in Paradise.

DAVID BEN-GURION

———————❧———————

*W*e are so old that in our history everything has happened and nothing new can occur.

MAX NORDAU

*W*ords are like medicine: measure them with care; an overdose can hurt.

SAYING

*H*e who is able to write a book and does not write it is as one who has lost a child.

RABBI NAHMAN OF BRATSLAV

*A*s long as I do not utter a word, I am its master; once I utter it, I am its slave.

ADAPTED FROM IBN GABIROL

———————

I'm not a philosopher – for that I'm too small.
I'm not a critic – for that I'm too big.

GEORG BRANDES

Man puts his hand to the flinty rock
   and overturns mountains by the roots.
He hews out channels in the rocks,
   and his eye sees every precious thing.
He binds up the flow of rivers,
   and what is hidden he brings to light.
But Wisdom, where may she be found,
   and where is the place of Understanding?
Man does not know her place,
   nor is she found in the land of the living.
The Deep says, 'Not in me,'
   the Sea says, 'Nor with me.'
She cannot be acquired for gold,
   and silver cannot be weighed as her
price . . .
For she is hidden from the eyes of all living
things,
   concealed even from the birds of the air.
Abaddon and Death say,
   'We have heard only her echo.'
But God understands her way
   and He knows her place,
For He looks to the ends of the earth
   and sees everything under the heaven.
When He gave the wind its weight
   and meted out the waters by measure,
when He made a law for the rain

and a way for the thunderbolt,
then He saw Wisdom, and described her;
He established her and searched her out.
But to man He said,
'To be in awe of the Lord – that is wisdom,
and to avoid evil – that is understanding.'

JOB

One can positively never be deceived if one mistrusts everything in the world, even one's own scepticism.

ARTHUR SCHNITZLER

History teaches us that men and nations behave wisely once they have exhausted all other alternatives.

ABBA EBAN

Intellectuals always have microscopes before their eyes.

ALBERT EINSTEIN

Everyone sits in the prison of his own ideas.

ALBERT EINSTEIN

When a bore leaves the room, you feel as if someone came in.

My labour's vain,
No wealth I gain.
My fate since birth
Is gloom on earth.

If I sold shrouds,
No one would die.
If I sold lamps,
Then in the sky,
The sun for spite
Would shine by night.

ABRAHAM IBN EZRA

———————————

A shlemiel rushes to throw a drowning man
a rope – both ends.

When a shlimazl kills a chicken – it walks;
when he winds a clock – it stops.

When it rains gold, it is the fate of the
shlimazl to be under a roof.

The he shlemiel *is the pants presser who always drops the hot iron off the ironing board. The* shlimazl *is the shmo on whose foot the iron always falls. And the* Kibitser *is the one who says 'Tsk, tsk!'*

A nebech *is the one in a group you always forget to introduce.*

A *nebbech* and a *nudnik* were out walking when it began to drizzle. The *nudnik* said to the *nebbech*, 'Why don't you open your umbrella?'

'It won't help,' replied the *nebbech*.

'Why not?' moaned the *nudnik*.

'It's got holes in it!'

'Then why did you bring it?' asked the *nudnik*.

'I didn't think it would rain.'

Mr Shapiro was depressed. He never had girlfriends, no one understood his jokes or paid attention to his opinions. When he was invited to parties, even the host would forget his name in introductions. So he decided that he would do something to impress his neighbours and ensure him of a stream of party invitations.

The next day he rented a camel from the local circus, put on his khaki shorts and a pith helmet, mounted his camel and set forth on Hampstead High Street. Everywhere people stopped, buzzed, gawked and pointed.

For a week, Shapiro rode his trusty steed. One day, he parked the camel outside the Post Office, and when he came out, the camel had gone. At once, he went to the police station to report the disappearance.

'Camel?' repeated the sergeant,'You want to report a missing camel? What make of car is a camel, sir?'

'A *camel* camel, stupid. An animal!' cried Shapiro.

'Aha – I'll have to fill out a missing animal form, sir. How tall was the camel?'

'Um, from the pavement to his back, where I sat, a good seven feet.'

'What colour is the camel, sir?'

'Camel coloured, of course!'

'How many humps?'

'Can't remember – between one and three.'

'Oh dear sir, this really isn't a very adequate description. Is there anything else you can tell me about the camel?'

'Yes, yes, he is definitely, *definitely* male.'
'Well, sir, you are certainly adamant about that. How come you're so sure?'
'Because every time I rode on the camel, I could hear people yelling, "Hey, just look at the schmuck on that camel! !" '

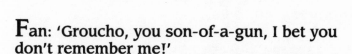

Fan: 'Groucho, you son-of-a-gun, I bet you don't remember me!'
Groucho Marx: 'Sir, I never forget a face – but in your case I'll be glad to make an exception.'

While out walking, Rubin stumbled on a stone and fell over a precipice. As he fell he grabbed hold of a branch on a tree growing off the cliffside.

'Please Lord,' he whispered, paralysed with fear, 'Lord, if you're listening, if there's *anyone* up there, please come and save me.'

Suddenly a voice boomed out, 'I'm here, Rubin, don't worry, your prayers will be answered and my palm will support you and bring you up to us.'

A long pause followed before Rubin said, 'Excuse me, but is there anybody else up there?'

*T*he fundamental evil of the
world arose from the fact that
the good Lord had not created
enough money.

HEINRICH HEINE

G-d loves the poor and helps the rich.

SAYING

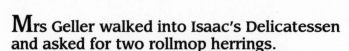

Mrs Geller walked into Isaac's Delicatessen and asked for two rollmop herrings.

'That will be £1.20 please Mrs Geller.'

'£1.20!' gasped Mrs Geller. 'Shlomo's Delicatessen, across the road, sells rollmops at 40p each – not 60p.'

'Nu,' said Isaacs. 'So buy your rollmops across the road.'

'I can't,' said Mrs Geller. 'He's sold out.'

'Hah!' said Isaacs. 'If I'd sold out I'd also sell rollmops at 40p each!'

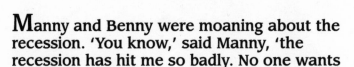

Manny and Benny were moaning about the recession. 'You know,' said Manny, 'the recession has hit me so badly. No one wants to buy any more.'

'Don't I know it,' replied Benny. 'My business is so atrocious that I can't stop worrying. You know, Manny, for the past month I've been sleeping like a baby.'

'A baby?' repeated Manny.

'Yes, a baby. I fall asleep and every two hours I wake up crying!'

We were awfully poor. But we had a lot of things that money can't buy – like unpaid bills.

BARBRA STREISAND

It's not that it is so good with money, but that it's so bad without it.

SAYING

The Cohens had just moved into their dream house in Stanmore. Trudy wanted the best décor, whatever the cost. So, she called the Queen's interior designer and requested a consultation.

The next day, one of the designers came over to the Cohens'. He asked Trudy what period she preferred and she said she didn't know. He said, 'Would you like a modern home?'

'No!'

'Italian provincial?'

'No!'

After naming five other period styles, he said, 'Mrs Cohen, I'm sorry, but the entire Royal Family are more helpful. If you want my help, you're going to have to give me an indication of the period.'

'Look, let's put it this way, I want this place to be so luxurious, so *dazzling*, that when my friends walk in they should take one look . . . and drop dead. Period.'

Were the rich but able to hire others to die for them then the poor would be making a real nice living.

SAYING

Shlomo was in the schmutter trade, but try as he might, he could not sell to the buyer of a large department store. Each month he would visit the buyer with new materials, but the notoriously anti-semitic buyer would shake his head, saying 'Sorry, but we always buy our materials from Browns or Windsors.'

On one occasion, the buyer decided to have a small joke with Shlomo, so, with much winking and nudging of his colleagues, he said to Shlomo, 'We've decided to place an order with you, Mr Gluckstein. We'll buy a length of the crushed velvet.'

'Wonderful, sir,' replied Shlomo. 'What length do you want?'

'From the tip of your nose to the tip of your penis!' laughed the buyer. 'Oh, and don't forget to include the bill with our *massive* order. We'll pay you instantly.'

A week later yards and yards of crushed velvet arrived at the department store, with an unbelievable bill. The buyer immediately phoned Shlomo.

'Mr Gluckstein, you seem to have misunderstood. I ordered the velvet to be the length between the tip of your nose and the tip of your penis. What is the meaning of this ridiculous amount and bill? !'

'I'm sorry, sir,' replied Shlomo, 'but you seem to have misunderstood. Maybe I should explain . . . the tip of my penis . . . well, it's somewhere in Poland!'

Solly Green was in court to become a British citizen.

'Before we grant you citizenship,' said the judge, 'I need to know that you are interested in Great Britain and our rulers. The first question is . . . what are the two main political parties of this nation?'

'A working man should have such time for parties!' answered Solly.

'All right then . . . who is John Major?'

'What sort of question is that? Doesn't everyone know?'

'Mr Green,' snapped the judge. 'Do you always have to answer a question so ambiguously?'

'Why not?'

'Mr Green,' shouted the judge. 'Just answer this – do you swear your undying allegiance to our Queen Elizabeth II, the future King Charles and all the Royal Family?'

'You want me to swear in court?'

'Please, please, *please*, Mr Green. Answer my questions with an answer not another question. Do you promise to support the Prime Minister of the country and the Government?'

'Your honour,' replied Solly. 'Is it not enough for you that I support a wife and eight children? You want my blood as well?'

Desperate Shlomo Kaplan stays in the synagogue after the evening prayer and, when everybody else has left, approaches the Holy Ark, opens the doors and cries, 'Dear Almighty, we are so poor, my children are hungry, my wife is sick – please help me. Tomorrow they announce the winner of the lottery – $2 million. Let me be the winner, please, and I'll give half to charity.'

Next day it is announced that no one has won and so the next lottery prize draw will be double.

So now Kaplan spends every night at the synagogue, at the Ark, begging and pleading with the Almighty, but at the next lottery draw once again there's no winner.

The big prize grows to $10 million and Kaplan is beside himself with desperation. He sleeps in the synagogue, and all day and all night without ceasing he begs the Almighty to let him win.

The night before the big lottery draw takes place, Kaplan opens the doors to the Ark once more and cries, '$10 million and I promise $5 million will go to charity – please let me win.'

A voice comes out of the Ark and says, 'Kaplan, Kaplan, I really want you to win, but please meet me half-way and buy a lottery ticket!'

Al Jolson had a bit of a problem with his father:

  'I bought my father an overcoat for $200, but I knew he'd be horrified at the cost so I told him I got it for $10! He rang me a few days later, very excited. "Guess what! That coat you got me for $10 I just sold it for $25. Can you get me a dozen more?" '

Every man has the right to be conceited until he is successful.

BENJAMIN DISRAELI

Morry Jacobs was swimming in the sea, when a huge wave swept him away 'Help! Help!' cried Morry.'I'm drowning, help! help!'

A lifeguard spotted Morry and dived in to save him. Eventually he reached the old man, gripped him across the chest and swam back holding on to Morry. When they reached the shore the lifeguard gave Morry mouth-to-mouth resuscitation. Ten minutes later Morry was breathing normally and the lifeguard helped him to get up. 'Now take it easy, sir,' said the lifeguard. 'I suggest you go back to your hotel and have a rest.'

Morry turned to an onlooker and whispered, 'Excuse me, could you help me with something?'

'Sure,' said the woman.

'Exactly how much do you tip for a thing like that?'

I moved into a new apartment. I had to give the landlord three hundred dollars for the first month's rent, three hundred dollars for the last month's rent, and three hundred dollars for security. Does this make sense? I give this man nine hundred dollars and he wants references from me. I should get references from him. Am I going to steal his apartment? Where would I hide it?

JACKIE MASON

When is a pauper miserable?
When he is invited to two weddings in one day.

Toil not to become rich, nor seek needless wealth;
Scarcely have you set your eye upon it, when it is gone!
For riches make themselves wings,
Like an eagle that flies toward the heavens.

PROVERBS

On his deathbed, Jack, an atheist, asked his three business partners, Moishe, Morris and Mo, to come to the hospital.

'Friends, my colleagues, I want you all to grant me a last wish.'

'Yes?' asked his partners.

'As you all know, I have no family and no heirs. I am dividing my wealth equally between the three of you. But out of respect, at my funeral, I want each of you to put a thousand pounds on my coffin before it is lowered into the ground.'

A few days later, Jack passed away. At the funeral service, his three partners approached the coffin before it was lowered. Moishe placed an envelope containing one thousand pounds on the coffin. Morris did likewise. Finally Mo went to the coffin, took both envelopes and replaced them with a cheque for three thousand pounds.

———————

My folks were poor, but I didn't mind poverty. They always played games. For instance, when I'd come home, they had moved.

JOEY BISHOP

When Michael Stein wandered into a pet shop in Petticoat Lane, he was astonished to hear a whisper.

'Psst, psst!' said the parrot, 'My name is Moshe and not only can I speak but I can also pray in Hebrew. I'm a really good buy.'

Michael took him home and told his friends.

'Oh yeh, yeh, yeh!' replied his friends. 'We'll bet you anything that your parrot can't utter a word of Hebrew, let alone pray.'

Before taking the parrot to the synagogue, the men placed their bets. The odds were fifty to one against.

'Right then,' said Michael, 'Moshe, my parrot, pray!' Moshe remained still and silent. 'Well, go on, Moshe, don't be shy. Recite for us!'

But Moshe uttered not a syllable and Michael had to pay his friends. On the way home from the synagogue the parrot started to sing.

'Now you're singing,' hissed Michael, 'but in the synagogue you were absolutely dumb and I lost a lot of money.'

'Don't worry,' replied Moshe the parrot, 'just imagine what odds you'll get next time!'

According to the income tax investigation, America is the land of untold wealth.

EDDIE CANTOR

The heart grows hard quicker in riches than an egg in boiling water.

LUDWIG BORNE

One night Dannie is lying in bed, tossing and turning, until eventually his wife Ruthie can stand it no longer.

'Dannie, Dannie, what's bothering you? Why can't you sleep?'

'What's bothering me? I'll tell you what's bothering me. I owe our dear friend Kennie £5,000 and I promised to pay it back to him by tomorrow morning. He's counting on me, but I don't have £500, let alone £5,000, and I'm so worried about it.'

Ruthie picks up the bedside telephone and dials Kennie's number. 'Hello, is that you, Kennie? This is Ruthie, Dannie's wife here. I know it's three o'clock in the morning, but I just wanted to tell you that Dannie can't repay the £5,000 he owes you. He doesn't have any money. Goodnight.' And with that she puts the phone down.

Dannie is astonished. 'Ruthie! Why did you do that?'

'So you can go to sleep – now *he* can toss and turn.'

Unbeknownst to Mr Alfred, one of the richest men in the world, his personal assistant goes to a grand beach hotel, to pre-arrange the details for his boss's visit in two weeks' time.

'In two weeks' time?' says the hotel manager. 'Forget it. We're completely booked up for the rest of the year.'

'Don't be silly,' says Alfred's assistant, 'just cancel the bookings, name the sum you want and I'll give it to you in cash.'

'How many rooms will Mr Alfred need?'

'The entire first floor, and I'd like to see the rooms, please.'

On the way, the assistant tells the manager that Alfred likes red roses everywhere – in the foyer, in the corridors, in the bedrooms, in the bathrooms, in the sitting rooms – and that they are to be flown in from abroad, if necessary, no matter what the cost.

'The rooms are fine. Let's open the shutters and check the beach. Oh, it's gold sand. Alfred doesn't like gold sand – he prefers silver sand, so you'll have to truck in as much as you need to cover the whole beach no matter what the cost. The water is blue – that's fine. The sky is blue – that's fine. And the sun is shining – so that's all right. We'll just have to make one small adjustment. For as long as Alfred stays here, every morning we would like a plane to spray mist on the right-hand side of the hotel to create the illusion of a small white cloud. Just organize it no matter what the cost. You'll be paid cash, in advance.'

Two weeks later a short, plump man with a tiny case turns up at the reception desk. 'My name is Alfred,' he says. 'Do you have a vacancy for me?'

'Of course, sir, we can give you the entire first floor. Let me show you to your rooms.'

'Marvellous, that's just what I like, the entire first floor. Look at all these wonderful red roses in the foyer, in the corridors, everywhere. How amazing at this time of year when they're out of season. Oh, and red roses in my rooms as well. And look at the lovely silver sand on the beach, and the blue sea, and the blue sky and the sun shining, and – aah,' exclaimed Alfred with a tear in his eye, 'there is my small white cloud on the right-hand side. Well, I ask you – with all this, who needs money?'

───────✸───────

To sell something you have to someone who wants it – that is not business. But to sell something you don't have to someone who doesn't want it – *that* is business.

JAMES SELIGMAN

Most people, when in prosperity, are so overbrimming with wisdom (however inexperienced they may be), that they take every offer of advice as a personal insult. Whereas in adversity they know not where to turn, but beg and pray for counsel from every passer-by.

BARUCH SPINOZA

'So, how are things in the legal profession these days?' asked Harry.

'Terrible,' replied Maurice. 'Things have got so bad that last week I told my wife I wanted a divorce. Now, at least I have a case.'

Sarah and Rebecca are having lunch one day at the 21 Club in New York and Sarah is recounting how well her husband has been doing lately.

'He bought me this diamond ring. It cost $200,000.'

'Fant*aaa*stic!' enthuses Rebecca.

'And what do you think of these earrings he bought me? They cost $300,000,' says Sarah.

'Fant*aaa*stic!'

'And when we came back from our world cruise, he surprised me with this wonderful brooch, which cost $500,000.'

'Fant*aaa*stic!'

'Well, that's enough about me. How are you doing, Rebecca?'

'We can't complain. We're doing so well that my husband says I'm not up to the standards required in our milieu and so he's paid for me to go to a charm school.'

'A charm school?' says Sarah surprised. 'What do you learn in a charm school?'

'The first thing you learn,' replies Rebecca, 'is to say "fant*aaa*stic" instead of "bullshit".'

Moussaieff, when asked about his business, said, 'Well, I'm not a jewellery salesman. What I do when someone comes into my shop is to assess how much money he's got and what is the nicest way of transferring what is in his pocket into mine.'

Rich people swell up with pride.
Poor people swell up with hunger.

SHOLOM ALEICHEM

Two traders who made the rounds of provincial markets selling the same merchandise, met on the station platform.

'So, Levine, where are you heading?'

'Me?' answered Levine. 'I'm going to Manchester.'

'Hh!' snorted his competitor. 'You tell me you are going to Manchester because you want me to believe you are going to Liverpool. But I know you really *are* going to Manchester, so why do you tell me a lie?'

Jack was telling his friend Sam about his four sons.

'Sam, I tell you, my boys, they are all intellectuals – they're all doctors.'

'Doctors?'

'Yes. David is a playwright, he's a doctor of literature. Michael is a poet, he's a doctor of philosophy. Alan is an anthropologist, he's a doctor of human science. And Johnny's a composer, he's a doctor of music.'

'So, Jack, what have you been doing all these years?'

'Ach, I'm, just a businessman. My factory isn't that big, but thank the Lord it brings in enough for me to support all of them.'

Benjamin Disraeli's definition of Lawyers:
'Ever illustrating the obvious, explaining the
evident – and expatiating the
commonplace.'

*It is a great thing to make a fortune. There is
only one thing greater, and that is to keep it
when made.*

BENJAMIN DISRAELI

*My filing system is my brain and my waste
paper basket.*

SIR ISAAC WOLFSON

A man walked into a menswear store.

'Mr Josephs,' said the owner, Monty. 'You've come to the best store. We are a top class East End tailor. No bargaining, schbargaining at Monty's Menswear.'

'Good!' replied Mr Josephs. 'I don't like all the bartering that normally goes on.'

'Oh, Mr Josephs, I totally understand. Now, I'm not going to give you this wonderful suit for two hundred pounds, not even for one hundred and eighty but one hundred and seventy-five pounds.'

'What a pleasure to be here at Monty's Menswear,' said Mr Josephs. 'I'm not going to insult you and offer one hundred and twenty. Nor will I waste your time with one hundred and forty. I'll give you one hundred and fifty pounds for that suit!'

'It's yours for one hundred and sixty!'

'Wonderful! I'll take it!'

———————❦———————

'I don't understand, David. Why is it that your firm is called McDonald, Brown and Levene, when McDonald is retired and Brown has never won a case. Everyone knows that the firm's success is down to you.'

'You've forgotten something,' laughed David Levene.

'What's that?' asked his friend.

'My clients read from right to left!'

Mr Cohen spoke no English when he left Poland to come to England. Opening his first bank account, he signed his name with two crosses. Years later, he decided to open a savings account for his acquired wealth. This time he signed with three crosses.

'Mr Cohen, there's a slight discrepancy in your signature,' said the clerk. 'Could you explain this to us?'

'Of course,' replied Cohen. 'It's my wife! You know what they're like! You get rich and all of a sudden they want you to have a middle name!'

Business is:
1. Bad! 'He earns and I lose.'
2. Fair! 'Both of us earn.'
3. Good! 'I earn and he loses.'

SHOLOM ALEICHEM

Lawyers are like doctors. Every one's a specialist and when they don't know the answer, they'll start talking to you in Latin.'

ALAN KING

Americans are getting stronger. Twenty years ago, it took two people to carry ten dollars' worth of groceries. Today, a five-year-old can do it.

HENNY YOUNGMAN

'You're just not flash enough,' said Lennie to his friend Alan. 'With your wealth, you should travel in luxury. Get rid of that old Volvo. Buy yourself a brand new Rolls-Royce with a telephone, bar, fridge, TV and video. Then you'll really impress your clients. And don't forget to hire a chauffeur as well!'

Alan agreed. Now that he had become a millionaire, he had to spruce up his image.

A few weeks later Alan was travelling on the North Circular, when he saw Lennie's Rolls-Royce in front. Immediately, he phoned Lennie's car phone, but was surprised to hear a strange voice on the other end.

'I'm sorry, sir, but Mr Goldblum is unavailable to take your call right now,' said Lennie's chauffeur.

'Tell him it's urgent,' said Alan. 'Tell him it's his old friend Alan Bernbaum.'

Eventually, Lennie came to the phone.

'So, Alan, what do you want?' asked Lennie.

'Lennie, I had to tell you that I took your advice. See the Rolls behind you? Well it's mine and I'm inside, being driven by Paul, my chauffeur. I'm watching a great movie, drinking a glass of scotch and eating a huge salt beef sandwich. Well Lennie, what do you think now?'

'It's great, Al, but for this you got me out of my shower?'

*When hen things don't get better, don't worry –
they may get worse.*

SAYING

———————◆———————

My doctor is wonderful. Once in 1955,
when I couldn't afford an operation, he
touched up the X-rays.

JOEY BISHOP

———————◆———————

'Business is terrible, absolutely terrible.
Every day I open my store I lose money.'
  'So how do you make a living?'
  'On the sabbath, when it's closed.'

—————————————

Robber: Your money or your life?
Jack Benny: I'll have to think it over!

———————————————

How do you make a small fortune in Israel?
Bring a big fortune.

Joe Jolstein, theatrical agent, was staring out his window wondering if he'd get another booking that month, when suddenly he heard someone walking towards his office door.

He grabbed the phone and started talking: 'Hey, Gazza, I've got a football promotion for you . . . yeah, ten thousand . . . no problem . . .'

There was a knock on the door and a man came in. Joe waved him to take a seat, and carried on talking.

'. . . And did I tell you I've got Bobby de Niro for Henry Higgins in *My Fair Lady?* Yes, and Liza . . . yes, yes, Liza Minnelli . . . she's doing that new Mother Teresa play for me . . . Look, I've got to go, I've got another client with me. Give me a bell next week . . . and good luck in the Cup Final.'

He put down the phone and said to the man: 'Have a cigar, young man, and tell me what I can do for you.'

'Um . . .' replied the man, 'Actually I've come to reconnect your phones . . .'

An insurance company has a court order
restraining me from mentioning its name.
I've got so many policies with this company,
when I leave for the office in the morning,
my wife tells me, 'Have a nice day, darling.
Take chances!'

ALAN KING

David met Jonathan at the deli and offered
him a parrot – a very unusual parrot, fluent
in three languages, it could even sing.
   'I don't really need a parrot,' said
Jonathan, 'but I might give it to a friend as
a present. How much is it?'
   '£500,000,' replied David, without batting
an eyelid.

'£500,000? Forget it!'

A week later they met again in the same deli.

'Well, David, have you sold your miraculous parrot?' asked Jonathan.

'You'll be surprised, but I did.'

'For £500,000?'

'I sure did.'

'You mean you got £500,000 in *cash* for it?'

'Not cash, but I got two Siamese cats worth £250,000 each.'

Two Jewish mothers met in the street.

'Miriam, I've heard your Josh has left accountancy,' said Sarah.

'Yes. But Sarah is he doing well. He's become a salesman.

'A salesman! Is he any good?'

'Good? My Josh is a *superb* salesman. Only last week a woman came in to buy a suit to bury her husband in. And d'you know what? Josh persuaded her to buy an extra pair of trousers!'

In the 1920s in Warsaw young Jacob informed his family that he's decided to emigrate to the Holy Land. His mother and father try very hard to persuade him that this desert land so far away from Poland is not the right place for their beloved son. But Jacob insists that this is the only place for Jews, that this is his dream land and he absolutely *has* to go. So they give him a substantial amount of their hard-earned zlotys and Jacob goes on his way.

A month later a letter arrives in Warsaw:

Dear Mum and Dad,

I can't tell you how happy I am in this first Jewish city of Tel Aviv. It's only a small city – in fact, there's one street with sand dunes on the right, dunes on the left, dunes behind and dunes in front. Blue skies up above and the sun shines all day – indeed it's unusually warm. Yes, and I'd like to thank you very much for the zlotys you gave me and to tell you how well I have spent your money. I have just opened the first snow skiing equipment shop here in town and I'm very proud of it.

Your loving son,
Jacob

His father replied:

Dear Jacob,

I'm glad you're so happy, but, upon receiving this letter, please, the first thing you must do is to sell the shop immediately.

Never mind how little you get for it – just sell it.

Your loving,
Dad

One month later:
Dear Dad,

Thanks for your letter. I did exactly as you told me, but, alas, I couldn't get a penny for the shop. I lost all your hard-earned zlotys, but not for the reason you thought. It is because of the competition.

Your loving son,
Jacob

Small child: What does two times two make?
Lew Grade: Buying or selling?

*S*how business is 98% luck and 2% talent.

BUD FLANAGAN

Acting is all about honesty. If you can fake that, you've got it made.

GEORGE BURNS

At a New York function Muhammad Ali was introduced to violinist Isaac Stern.

'You might say we're in the same business. We both earn a living with our hands,' said Stern.

'You must be pretty good,' replied the boxer.'There isn't a mark on you.'

Reminiscing about his act as a child with George Jessel and Walter Winchell in vaudeville, Eddie Cantor told Jack Benny:

'We had a great cast. Walter Winchell, George Jessel, me and twelve girls. Winchell was ambitious. Even then he always had a typewriter in his room. I was ambitious, too. I always had schoolbooks in my dressing-room.'

'And what about Jessel?'

'He was the most ambitious,' replied Cantor. 'He had the twelve girls in his room.'

When Samuel Goldwyn informed an aide that he wanted to make a film of the book *The Well of Loneliness*, he was told,

'Admittedly, it is a bestseller. But you can't make a film out of it . . . it's about . . . lesbians.'

'Big deal,' replied Goldwyn. 'So, make them Latvians.'

I'll give it to you in two words: im possible.

SAMUEL GOLDWYN

Samuel Goldwyn told one of his scriptwriters,
  'When I want your opinion, I'll give it to you!'

The wide screen will make bad films twice as bad.

SAMUEL GOLDWYN

Gentlemen, I have made up my mind. Include me out.

SAMUEL GOLDWYN

When the director of the 1936 movie, *Dodsworth*, mentioned to Samuel Goldwyn that he thought parts of the story were too caustic, Goldwyn replied,
  'To hell with the cost, we're going ahead.'

Comedy, like sodomy, is an unnatural act.

MARTY FELDMAN

Question: What do you need to be a good comic?
Answer: You need to be tall and slim, or short and fat – or to be talented.

Commenting on his father's ownership of cinemas, Lord Bernstein admitted, 'I was born with a silver screen in my mouth.'

When he received his OBE at Buckingham Palace, Bud Flanagan said to Prince Philip: 'You've got a smashing house here for a matinée.'

In a letter to Sam Zolotow, Groucho Marx wrote: 'My plans are still in embryo. In case you've never been there, this is a small town on the outskirts of wishful thinking.'

This is a man who has not let success go to his head – a man who is humble and unspoiled. He is as unassuming, as comfortable to be with as an old glove – and just about as interesting.

GROUCHO MARX at S J Perelman's testimonial dinner

I have no advice to give to young struggling actors. To young struggling actresses, my advice is to keep struggling. If you struggle long enough you will never get in trouble, and if you never get in trouble, you will never be much of an actress.

GROUCHO MARX

Fan: It's a real pleasure for me to meet Groucho Marx.
Groucho: I've known him for years, and I can tell you it's not much of a pleasure.

An amateur thinks it's funny if you dress a man up as an old lady, put him in a wheelchair, and give the wheelchair a push that sends it spinning down a slope towards a stone wall. For a pro, it's got to be a real old lady.

GROUCHO MARX

An actress, notorious for rolling her 'R's said to director and composer Jerome Kern, 'You want me to cr-r-r-r-r-ross the stage. How can I get acr-r-r-r-r-ross?'

'My dear,' replied Kern, 'why don't you just roll on your r-r-r-r-rs? !'

When he was in Hollywood, the old vaudevillian, Jesse Block, looked up Fanny Brice and reminded her that they had appeared together at the Oriental Theatre in Chicago.

'I never played the Oriental,' said Miss Brice.

'We did,' replied Block. 'And after the show we went to the College Inn.'

'I never went to the College Inn.'

'And I pointed out Al Capone to you – surely you remember that?'

'Who's Al Capone?' she persisted.

'Fanny, that was the week that you got $7,500 at the Oriental.'

'I did not,' retorted Miss Brice. 'I got $8,000.'

The great violinist, Isaac Stern, was asked for his opinions on other 'great' violinists such as Jack Benny.

'Well,' said Stern. 'When Jack Benny walks out in tails in front of ninety great musicians, he looks like the world's greatest violinist. It's a shame he has to play.'

If it isn't a Stradivarius,' said Benny, 'I've been robbed of a hundred and ten dollars.

When Benny played in Hollywood, Zubin Mehta, the Israeli conductor, commented, 'Throughout Jack's violin solo at the Hollywood Bowl the audience were glued to their seats ... that was the only way he could get them to sit down!'

When he received a national award, Benny accepted the honour saying,

'I don't really deserve this beautiful award. But I have arthritis and I don't deserve that either.'

Jack Benny played Mendelssohn last night. Mendelssohn lost.

In 1963, as Jack Benny was performing in Pittsburgh, news came through that his wife, Mary, had been held up in her New York suite and robbed of her jewellery and most treasured diamond ring. In a state of high anxiety Benny tried to call his wife at the hotel but was told she had gone out.

When he reached her, four hours later, Benny exclaimed, 'Mary, Mary, where on earth have you been?'

'At the jeweller's,' she replied, 'looking for another ring.'

'What!' cried Benny. 'At a time like this you're out shopping for a diamond?'

'Sure. It's like when you fall off a horse,' answered his wife. 'If you don't get right back on, you never ride again.'

Jack Benny was invited to the White House and arrived carrying his famous violin case. A guard asked him, 'Mr Benny, could you tell me what is in that case?'

'Only a machine gun,' replied Benny.

'Thank G-d, Mr Benny,' said the guard.'I was afraid you'd brought your violin.'

We owe a lot to Thomas Edison – if it wasn't for him, we'd be watching television by candlelight.

MILTON BERLE

In the Lower East Side, if you wanted to throw out your garbage, you opened a window, you threw out your garbage. Everybody knew that garbage was coming. You heard a window go up, it was like an air-raid siren. People walked around looking out for flying garbage. But in these new, fancy buildings, you don't throw garbage out of the window. You have to take it to an incinerator. You'll find that all of these incinerators have one thing in common – you can't throw any garbage in them! Because nothing fits in the incinerator. You have to make sure your garbage is small. When I go to buy something, I don't care if it fits in the house – I make sure it fits in the incinerator. And you can't throw nothing in the incinerator even if it does fit because the incinerator only allows you to throw out certain types of garbage. There's a list of certain garbage you're allowed to throw out. The rest of the garbage you're stuck with. In my building, the apartments are filthy – the incinerator is clean.

JACKIE MASON

*Y*ou don't have to be Jewish to be traumatized, but it helps.

WOODY ALLEN

At a time when the Russian military were kidnapping young Jewish boys and enlisting them into the Tsar's army, the first Lubavitcher rabbi was asked by his followers, 'What should a Jewish boy do to keep kosher when he's served non-kosher food?'

The rabbi said, 'Well, he should eat around it. He should eat the vegetables. He should eat a piece of bread, he should eat fruit.'

But what if there are no vegetables, no bread and no fruit?' asked his followers. 'Suppose that all he can get is a piece of pork?'

'Then he shouldn't eat it,' the rabbi told them. 'He can carry on for a few days, just drinking water.'

'But what if it's more than a few days? Let's say it's ten days, or two weeks. The boy will die. So, should he die or should he eat something to save his life?'

The rabbi thought and thought until he finally answered, 'Well, he should eat a little bit, in order not to die. But he should not lick his fingers afterwards.'

———————❧———————

How do you know Jesus was Jewish? He stayed at home till he was thirty, he worked in his father's business, his mother thought he was G-d, and he thought she was a virgin!

Other people have a nationality. The Irish and the Jews have a psychosis.

BRENDAN BEHAN

Elaine: That will be all now Deborah. No more Hebrew today – I've got a splitting headache.

Deborah: Oh, I know all about that. Moses had a headache too!

Elaine: Moses had a headache? Who told you that?

Deborah: My dad. He said that G-d gave Moses two tablets.

On his way home from the office, Jonathan always popped in to his local pub for a drink. One evening, in the course of a conversation, the barman asked Jonathan, 'What is it that makes Jews so smart?'

'It's the gefilte fish,' replied Jonathan.

'What's gelfilte fish?'

'Well,' said Jonathan, 'it's minced carp mixed with bread, onions and hard-boiled eggs, which are then made into fish cakes which you boil.'

'Really? Can I have some?'

'Come to my home next Friday night and I'll be delighted to serve you a piece of gefilte fish. It'll cost you a couple of pounds.'

So, on Friday night, the barman went to Jonathan's house and duly bought his piece of gefilte fish. He didn't like the taste at first, but he persevered because he wanted to improve himself.

The following Friday the barman did the same, and the week after that, and so on for five or six weeks, until one day at the bar he said to Jonathan, 'Am I not being cheated a bit by you charging me £2 for a little piece of gefilte fish that's supposed to make me clever?'

'You see how it works?' cried Jonathan. 'You're getting smarter already!'

Two Russian Jews were standing in a queue for bread.

'That's it,' said one to the other. 'I am sick of all these bloody queues. I'm going to shoot Yeltsin.'

Three hours later he returned and gloomily went back to his place in the queue.

'Well?' asked his friend. 'Did you kill him?'

'Not a chance. The queue was twice as long as this one!'

Since the Exodus, Freedom has always spoken with a Hebrew accent.

HEINRICH HEINE

Bernstein was on business and arrived at his hotel very late, to find that his room had been double-booked. Just as he was about to complain, a rather attractive businesswoman approached the counter. She had been booked into the same room as Bernstein and there were no other rooms available.

'Look, madam. I am very tired. Normally I would have left here to find another hotel, but it is now midnight and I must get some sleep.'

'I feel the same way,' replied the woman. 'Why don't we just share the room? It will be big enough.'

Slightly taken aback by this, Bernstein agreed with the idea.

Once they were in the room, Bernstein made a bed for himself in an armchair. The woman got into the large kingsize bed and turned out the light. Five minutes later, she turned it back on.

'Look, sir, you must be very tired and really uncomfortable in that chair. Why don't you come and lie down on the other side of the bed, and sleep there instead.'

Bernstein agreed. 'Oh this does feel much more comfortable. I really did need to lie down.'

'Listen,' said the woman. 'We don't know each other at all, but it's cold tonight, so why don't you get into the bed? You'll be much warmer under the blankets.'

'Good idea. Thanks very much,' said Bernstein.

'One more thing,' suggested the woman in a slightly huskier voice. 'You don't know me, I don't know you. Downstairs, no one knew us . . . so why don't we play around a little? Why don't we party a bit?'

'You really are terrific,' said Bernstein. 'You're so right. I don't know you, you don't know me and downstairs no one knows us. But just tell me one thing, *Who on earth will we invite?*'

'**M**y boy,' boasted Mr Shaw, 'has just graduated from Oxford University in PPE.'

'PPE?' asked his friend. 'What's PPE?'

'Politics, Philosophy and Economics, of course,' replied Mr Shaw.

'And what job has he got with this PPE degree?'

'Well,' said Mr Shaw, 'he's having problems getting a job – but at least he knows why he can't get one!'

Two Jews – one Polish, one Czechoslovakian – were walking through London Zoo and stopped to admire the bears. Suddenly, one of the bears reached out, grabbed the Czech and promptly ate him.

The Pole ran to the warden crying, 'Zat bear! It ate my friend!'

'Calm down, sir. I'll get your friend back for you,' said the warden. 'Just tell me, was it the male bear that ate him, or the female bear?'

'I think it was the male bear.'

So, the warden got his gun and shot the male bear. However, when they opened up the dead bear, there was no sign of the Czechoslovakian.

'Oy Vay!' cried the Pole. 'It must have been the female who ate him up!'

So, the warden shot the female and when they opened it up, sure enough the Czech was inside.

The moral of the story: Never trust a Polish Jew when he says the Czech's in the male!

Because there are nine million inhabitants in New York City of which three million are Jews, supposedly every third person you meet on the street is Jewish, but, in fact, every second one is because they move faster.

DOVALEH GOTTESMANN

'There are three kinds of Jews,' said eight-year-old Danny Shaw to his religious education class at school, 'Liberal, Reform and Orthodontists.'

Hymie Cohen wanted to join his local golf club, but when he applied for membership, his application was turned down on the grounds of his religion – 'No Jews admitted'.

On his letter of rejection there was a list of the committee members – Jackson, Fielding, Johnson, Gascoigne and Goldwater.

'You see,' said Hymie to his wife. 'There's a Goldwater. I'm going to phone him.'

A few minutes later Mr Goldwater's secretary told him that there was a Hymie Cohen on the phone. 'Yes, what can I do for you, Mr Cohen?' asked Mr Goldwater.

'Well, I want to join your golf club and they won't admit me because I'm Jewish. How come, Mr Goldvater, you're on the committee?'

'Mr Cohen. Let me tell you. I am not Mr Goldvater, nor am I Mr Goldwarter. I am Mr Goldwater, my father was Mr Goldwater and his father Olev Hasholem was Mr Goldwater!'

*T*zoress with soup are easier to swallow than tzoress without soup.

SAYING

Man cannot live without a lasting trust in something indestructible within him, but both his trust and its indestructible object can remain forever concealed from him. One expression of this concealment is man's faith in a personal G-d.

FRANZ KAFKA

———————— ✡ ————————

G-d, I know we are your chosen people, but once in a while couldn't you choose someone else?

SHOLOM ALEICHEM

A rabbi and a priest were discussing their promotion prospects.

'Are you ambitious for promotion?' asked the priest.

'Sometimes,' replied the rabbi. 'I often hope that I will be in charge of a larger congregation. What about you?'

'Well, I often dream about becoming a Cardinal.'

'And then?' asked the rabbi.

'Well, it's possible that I could become Pope one day!' laughed the priest.

'And then?' asked the rabbi.

'Well, I suppose that's it, unless you want me to become G-d! !'

'Nu,' said the rabbi. 'One of our boys did!'

Two unemployed rabbis were discussing their predicament.

'Fortunately, I have a part-time job,' said the first rabbi.

'That's something at least. What do you do?' said the other.

'I work on the assembly line in a battery factory.'

'In a battery factory? What do you do there?'

'Ach, I just wave my hand as the batteries go past, and say, "I wish you long life!" '

G-d is like a Jewish waiter, he has too many tables.

MEL BROOKS

Mr Cohen was on the bus home when he noticed a little old man sitting opposite, talking to himself and laughing out loud. Sometimes he would hold up his hand, stop talking and start again.

Eventually Cohen said to him, 'Excuse me, sir. Is anything the matter?'

'No, I'm fine. I like to tell myself jokes when I'm travelling.'

'But why do you raise your hand?'

'Oh, I do that to stop myself telling a joke I've already heard!'

'I'd love to come to your house-warming party, Erwin, but how do I get to your place?'

'Well, it's easy. It's on the corner of Hall Road. Go into the driveway and it's the second entrance. Ring the bell on the entryphone with your right elbow and, when you hear the buzzer, just push the door open with your left elbow. Then, press the button to call the lift with your right elbow. When the lift arrives, the door opens automatically – just hold it back with your left elbow. Press the button for the third floor with your right elbow. The door opens automatically again and on the right is flat 22. Press the doorbell with your left elbow. And there you are!'

'Thanks, that sounds pretty clear, but what's all this business with the elbows?'

'Well, you're not coming empty-handed, are you?'

Two Jews on an island will build three synagogues – one for each, and the third neither wants to attend.

SAYING

Mr Rappaport took his son Rubin to the circus. Rubin cheered throughout the show, but his father didn't seem to enjoy it very much.

At last it was time for Vic the Flying Violinist to perform his spectacular stunt. He walked across a tightrope holding a violin. At the other side, he climbed into a cannon and was fired into the air. As he came flying out he played music on his violin. The audience went wild, cheering and clapping. Rubin turned to his father:

'Wasn't that amazing, Dad?'

'Nu!' replied his father. 'A Menuhin he ain't!'

I believe in the sun even when it is not shining.
I believe in love even when not feeling it.
I believe in G-d even when He is silent.

Inscription on a cellar wall in Cologne where Jews hid from the Nazis

A vicar, a priest and a rabbi were discussing miracles over tea.

'Well,' said the vicar. 'I definitely believe in the concept of miracles. On a recent scout trip, one of our boys got into trouble in his canoe. He capsized and then suddenly, in the middle of nowhere, with no one around, a life jacket appeared in the water and the boy swam to safety.'

'I also believe in miracles,' said the priest. Last year on our church skiing trip, we were on a black slope and suddenly we heard a huge crash. There was an avalanche for the first time in thirty years. A massive rock was heading for our group and then suddenly, after I'd prayed to the Lord, the sun appeared, the avalanche disappeared and the rock stopped.'

'What wonderful experiences,' said the rabbi. 'I also have a story to tell. Last Saturday, after the Shabbat morning service, I was walking home and on the side of the road I caught sight of a suitcase. Inside there were stacks of ten-pound notes. Anyway, I was in a state of turmoil. You must know that on the Sabbath, we Jews are forbidden to carry, and especially not handle money. So I prayed for guidance. And then a miracle – suddenly it was Monday!'

Not only is there no G-d but try getting a plumber on weekends.

WOODY ALLEN

I landed at Orly airport and discovered my luggage wasn't on the same plane. My bags were finally traced to Israel where they were opened and all my trousers were altered.

WOODY ALLEN

Returning from Europe, Woody Allen had to pay high charges for his excess baggage.
   'Next time,' promised Allen, 'I'll fly El Al! The Israeli airline doesn't worry if you're overweight. They worry only if you're underweight!'

Two men were sitting in the same compartment of the Intercity to Manchester. One man, who was reading the *Jewish Chronicle*, said to the other, 'So . . . you're going to Manchester?'

The man put down his book. 'Yes,' he said, 'I am going to Manchester. My business is manufacturing. I manufacture ladies' jackets. Yes, I have a factory in the East End. My name is Harry Rosenblatt. I'm married to Beckie whose maiden name was Bloom. I belong to Golders Green United synagogue. I'm not rich. I live on the Finchley Road. I can't play golf. I play bridge at the Hendon Bridge Club. I spend a weekend every month visiting my son and his wife in Manchester. I vote Labour. I don't have a brother of the same name because, as far as I know, I've never had a brother. You don't know my sister either because she's been living in the States for the past forty years. And I think that's about it. So, if there are no more questions, can I return to my book, *please*? !'

A mute told a deaf man how a blind man saw a cripple run on water.

SAYING

If my relativity theory is verified, Germany will proclaim me a German and France will call me a citizen of the world. But if my theory is proved false, France will emphasize that I am a German and Germany will say that I am a Jew.

ALBERT EINSTEIN at the Sorbonne in 1932

You are the President of a nation of 150 million people. I am the President of a million presidents.

CHAIM WEIZMANN to President Truman

Asked what his handicap was, Sammy Davis Jnr replied, 'I'm a coloured, one-eyed Jew – do I need anything else?'

A rabbi and a priest were having breakfast. The priest ordered bacon and eggs and turned to the rabbi:

'Rabbi, when are you going to start enjoying some of this delicious bacon?'

'At your wedding!' replied the rabbi.

While on a cruise, Dorothy Parker found herself the object of an overbearing drunk's attention.

'I simply can't bear fools,' confided the drunk.

'Apparently,' replied Miss Parker, 'your mother did not have the same difficulty.'

Mr Shaw was concerned that his son at Oxford would forget the Day of Atonement, so he sent him a telegram:

YOM KIPPUR STARTS TOMORROW

His son telephoned him immediately.

'Thanks for the telegram, Dad. Do me a favour, put fifty quid for me on it to win!'

A Jew went into a kosher deli on the Lower East Side of New York and was absolutely amazed that his Chinese waiter spoke fluent Yiddish.

At the end of the meal, the Jew called the manager over.

'What a lovely meal, especially the gefilte fish and the salt beef.'

'Thank you, sir,' replied the manager.

'And tell me, how did you get a Yiddish-speaking Chinaman as a waiter?'

'Ssh!' whispered the manager. 'He thinks he's learning English!'

Due to the loss of an eye in the Second World War, the Israeli statesman Moshe Dayan had to wear an eyepatch. One day, after being stopped for speeding, he argued with the policeman, 'I have only one eye. What do you want me to watch – the speedometer or the road?'

Receptionist: McFarlane, Bloom and Singh. How can I help you?
Caller: Oh, hello. Can I speak to Michael Bloom?
Receptionist: I'm sorry, sir, but Mr Bloom isn't in today. This is Yom Kippur.
Caller: Well, Miss Kippur, would you tell him his car's ready?

*An opponent of David Ben-Gurion remarked,
'The difference between the Messiah and
Ben-Gurion is that the Messiah refuses to
come, and Ben-Gurion refuses to go.'*

*On a visit to California, David Ben-Gurion
told his hosts,
    'I envy your deserts – not just because they
are deserts but because you can afford to
keep them deserts.'*

A Russian immigrant was asked about his life in Jerusalem.

'How did you find living conditions over in Russia?'

'Thank G-d I couldn't complain,' he answered.

'And how do you find living conditions over here in Israel?'

'Thank G-d I *can* complain.'

Please accept my resignation. I don't want to belong to any club that will accept me as a member.

GROUCHO MARX to the Friar's Club in Hollywood

After she had kissed Omar Sharif in *Funny Girl*, Barbra Streisand was heard saying, 'Never mind what Nasser will say! You should have heard what my Aunt Rosie said!'

The Day of Atonement was drawing to a close. The congregation was tired and hungry after almost 23 hours of fasting and twelve hours of praying. Suddenly the rabbi announced he was too weak to lead the Concluding Service.

'Congregants, one of you must take over. We have to finish our prayers before we can go to our homes and break the fast. Now, who will volunteer?'

The congregation were silent. 'Please,' begged the rabbi. 'Won't anyone do this mitzvah?'

Still no one volunteered.

Eventually, someone put up his hand. 'Rabbi, I can help you!' said Mr Stern.

'Oh! thank you, Mr Stern,' gasped the rabbi. 'Please come up to the bimah.'

'Oh no,' said Stern, 'I can't lead, but I know someone who will – my dog, Cuthbert.'

The congregation laughed.

'Your *dog*, Cuthbert?' echoed the rabbi.

Once again the congregation laughed. However, five minutes later, when no one had stepped forth, the rabbi conceded. 'All right, Mr Stern, bring in Cuthbert, the dog.'

A few minutes later, Stern came in with Cuthbert, who was wearing a yarmulke (skull cap) and a tallis (prayer shawl). The dog began the service. He knew all the prayers which he piously rendered and sang the songs and psalms beautifully. The congregation were moved to tears. The final shofar blast was sounded and the

congregation rushed over to Mr Stern and
Cuthbert.

The rabbi spoke, 'Mr Stern, may I thank
you for bringing us such a wonderful
chazzan. I haven't heard such beautiful
chanting since my childhood in Minsk. Why
don't you get your dog to join the
Rabbinate?'

'You talk to him,' replied Mr Stern. 'He
wants to be an accountant!'

One day in a Chinatown restaurant, a Jew
went up to an Oriental man and poured
some noodles over his head.

'That's for Pearl Harbor,' said the Jew.

'But I'm Chinese!' cried the man.

'Chinese, Siamese, *Japanese*, you're all the
same!'

The Chinaman picked up his plate of
lemon chicken and threw it over the Jew.

'That's for sinking the *Titanic*,' shouted the
Chinaman.

'But the *Titanic* was sunk by an
iceberg . . .'

'Goldberg, Greenberg, iceberg . . .'

Israel is a country so tiny that there is no room to write its name on the world map.

It is the only country in the world which is financed by its taxpayers abroad.

It is a country of boundless boundaries.

It is a country where mothers learn the mother-tongue from their sons.

It is a country where the fathers ate sour grapes and the children's teeth are excellent.

It is a country where one writes Hebrew, reads English and speaks Yiddish.

It is a country where everybody has the right to speak his mind, but there is no law forcing anybody to listen.

It is a country where all the capital is concentrated in Jewish hands – and there is much grumbling because of this.

It is a country of elections but no choice.

It is a country which is an organic part of its trade unions.

It is a country where nobody wants to work, so they build a new town in three days and go idle the rest of the week.

It is a country which produces less than it eats, and yet, of all places, it is here that nobody has ever died of hunger.

It is a country where nobody expects miracles, but everybody takes them for granted.

It is a country where one calls ministers simply 'Moishe' – and then almost dies with the excitement of it.

It is a country whose survival is permanently endangered, and yet its inhabitants' ulcers are caused by the neighbours from upstairs.

It is the only country in which I could live. It is my country.

EPHRAIM KISHON

Early one Saturday, a rabbi, who was an avid golfer, woke up to a glorious morning. He was overcome with the desire to play a round of golf and decided, contrary to all religious rules, to play a round before anyone was up and still be in time for the Shabbat morning service.

Alone on the course, he teed up and drove off. He did the first hole which was par four, in three.

Meanwhile the Angel Gabriel pleaded with the Almighty to punish the rabbi, but the Almighty just smiled.

The second hole was accomplished in two.

Once again Gabriel pleaded that the rabbi should be punished for breaking the Sabbath.

On the next hole the rabbi got a hole in one, and on the next.

The heavens were in turmoil. 'Almighty, Almighty,' cried the Angel Gabriel. 'Why are you not punishing this sinner?'

'Gabriel, my angel,' laughed the Almighty. 'Isn't he punished enough? Just think, he will never be able to tell this to anyone!'

Before desegregation, Jewish comedian George Jessel took black singer Lena Horne to the Stork Club, which was notorious for its bigoted management. The head waiter informed Jessel that there were no free tables that night. Finally he asked,

'I'm sorry, Mr Jessel, who made the reservation?'

'Abraham Lincoln!' replied the comedian. They got a table.

If we lose this war, I'll start another in my wife's name.

MOSHE DAYAN, during the Six Day War

*P*alestine has the size of a county and the problems of a continent.

ARTHUR KOESTLER

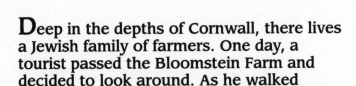

Deep in the depths of Cornwall, there lives a Jewish family of farmers. One day, a tourist passed the Bloomstein Farm and decided to look around. As he walked through the gate, he met Mrs Bloomstein.

'Come in and see our special cattle,' said Mrs Bloomstein.

Intrigued by the proposition of seeing a special breed, the tourist followed Mrs Bloomstein.

'Here are our exclusive cows,' boasted Mrs Bloomstein.

'Gosh,' said the tourist. 'What breed are they exactly?'

'Well, they're a cross between a Guernsey and a Holstein . . . known as the Goldsteins.'

'Wow!' cried the tourist. 'And tell me, do they have any unique characteristics?'

'Well, not really,' replied Mrs Bloomstein, 'there's only one small difference. Instead of saying moo, the Goldstein says nuu . . . nuu!'

Learning! Learning! Learning! That is the secret of Jewish survival.

ACHAD HA'AM

During the Vietnam War, President Nixon and Golda Meir were discussing their armies' strengths.

'Do you think we could swap generals?' asked Nixon.

'Which ones would you want?' replied Meir.

'General Rabin and General Dayan,' said the American. 'Which of our generals would you want?'

The Israeli Premier thought for a moment. 'General Motors and General Electric!'

*A*nyone who goes to a psychiatrist ought to have his head examined.

SAMUEL GOLDWYN

At thirteen, subject to the
   commandments;
At fifteen, the study of Talmud;
At eighteen, marriage;
At twenty, the pursuit [of a livelihood];
At thirty, the peak of strength;
At forty, wisdom;
At fifty, able to give counsel;
At sixty, old age creeping on;
At seventy, fullness of years;
At eighty, the age of 'strength';
At ninety, body bent;
At a hundred, as good as dead and gone
   completely out of the world.

RABBI JUDAH BEN TEMA, in *Ethics of the Fathers*

A man should live if only to satisfy his curiosity.

SAYING

Experimental Psychologist: A scientist who
                          pulls habits
                          out of rabbits.

L L LEVINSON

*Neurotics build castles in the air,
psychotics live in them, and
psychiatrists collect the rent.*

SAYING

A psychiatrist received a postcard from one of his patients on holiday in Israel:
   Having a wonderful time! Wish you were here to tell me why!

'Tell me, Dovid, what's the difference between a psychotic and a neurotic?'
   'Easy,' replied Dovid. 'A psychotic *thinks* that 2 plus 2 makes 5. A neurotic *knows* that 2 plus 2 makes 4 – but he just can't stand it!'

Doctor: Goldstein, is there any medical reason why you should not be drafted into the army?
Goldstein: Many, many doctor. For a start, half of my insides are missing.
Doctor: My word! What exactly is the nature of your problem?
Goldstein: No guts!

The ward phone rang. Nurse Jerome picked up the receiver.

'Hello,' said a voice on the other end of the phone. 'I'm calling about a patient of yours, Mr Goldstein. That's G-o-l-d-s-t-e-i-n.'

'Ah yes,' replied the nurse, 'Mr Goldstein. He had his operation on Thursday.'

'Could you tell me how Mr Goldstein is, please?' asked the caller.

'He's fine,' replied the nurse. 'In fact he should be discharged in a couple of days' time.'

'Thank you, nurse. And is he now allowed to eat what he wants?'

'Oh yes, Mr Goldstein is well enough to eat a big box of chocolates now,' laughed the nurse. 'So, sir, who can I say called?'

'No one. *I'm* Mr Goldstein. That doctor doesn't tell me a bloody thing!'

Do not sit too much, for sitting aggravates haemorrhoids;
Do not stand too much, for standing hurts the heart;
Do not walk too much, for walking hurts the eyes.
So, spend one third of your time sitting, one third standing, and one third walking.

TALMUD

'You really do look terrible, Mr Marks,' said the doctor. 'Tell me, do you drink?'

'Yes, only a bottle of scotch a day!'

'Oh dear!' gasped the doctor. 'You don't smoke as well, do you?'

'Well, maybe a few – about two packets a day.'

'This really is terrible, Mr Marks. What is your working day like?'

'Um . . . not bad. I get to the office at about 7 am and leave at 9 pm.'

'Mr Marks,' said the doctor, 'your life has too many stresses. You must stop smoking, stop drinking and work fewer hours. At this rate you're sure to have a heart attack. And, before you go, that'll be fifty pounds for my advice.'

'Nu?' replied Marks. 'So, who's taking it?'

When you need a physician, you esteem him a god;
When he has brought you out of danger, you consider him a king.
When you have been cured, he becomes human like yourself;
When he sends you the bill, you think him a devil.

JEDADIAH BEN ABRAHAM BEDERSI

The purpose of maintaining the body in good health is to make it possible for you to acquire wisdom.

MAIMONIDES

Mrs Bloom picked up the phone. At the other end was Mr Bloom's doctor.

'Mrs Bloom,' said the doctor. 'We've made a terrible mistake. We mixed up your husband's test results. He has either got Alzheimer's disease, or Aids.

'What!' cried Mrs Bloom.

'I tell you what,' said the doctor, 'send your husband out for a walk. If he comes back – don't sleep with him!'

So appreciate your vigor in the days of your
    youth, before those days of sorrow come
    and those years arrive of which you will
    say, 'I have no pleasure in them'; before
    sun and light and moon and stars grow
    dark, and the clouds come back again
    after the rain:
When the guards of the house become
    shaky,
And the men of valor are bent,
And the maids that grind, grown few, are
    idle,
And the ladies that peer through the
    windows grow dim,
And the doors to the street are shut –
With the noise of the hand mill growing
    fainter,
And the song of the bird growing feebler,
And all the strains of music dying down;
When one is afraid of heights
And there is terror on the road . . .
Before the silver cord snaps
And the golden bowl crashes,
The jar is shattered at the spring,
And the jug is smashed at the cistern.
And the dust returns to the ground
As it was,
And the life breath returns to God
Who bestowed it.

ECCLESIASTES

Erez Bendov was a pilot. He was an extremely handsome man and kept his body in shape and well tanned. It was time for his annual medical, so he went to see the company doctor.

'So, Mr Bendov, how are you feeling?'

'Fine, thank you doctor.'

'Do you smoke?'

'Maybe one cigar a month.'

'And alcohol?'

'I sometimes have a glass of wine if I'm eating out.'

'How are you sleeping?'

'Very well.'

'Any eye strain or headaches?'

'Nope.'

'Do you suffer from tension?'

'No.'

'Not even when you're taking off or landing a plane?'

'Not that I can recall. In fact, doctor, I think I am a very calm man indeed.

'Finally, Mr Bendov, I have to ask you a slightly personal question . . . about sexual activity. When was the last time you had sex with a woman?'

'Um . . . about 1955,' replied the pilot.

'What?' cried the doctor. 'That's a very long time ago Captain. I have to say the length of time astounds me!'

The pilot looked surprised. 'Hardly a long time, doctor,' he said, looking at his watch. 'Why . . . it's only 20.05 now!'

As the waves crashed around the Bournemouth coast, Benny Jacobs was pulled out of the raging waters by the lifeguard. His wife went running over sobbing, 'Benny, Benny, my baby! What happened?'

'Madam, please don't get hysterical,' said the lifeguard. 'Now, if you could clear a space for the doctor.'

At that moment the doctor appeared and told the lifeguard, 'Get everyone to stand back. I'm going to give this man artificial respiration.'

'What!' shrieked Benny's wife. 'My Benny gets real respiration or nothing!'

Life is the cheapest bargain – you get it for nothing.

SAYING

There are eight things that taken in large quantities are bad, but in small quantities are helpful:

Travel, sex, wealth, work, wine, sleep, hot baths and bloodletting.

TALMUD

My doctor told me I had low blood pressure, so he gave me my bill. That raised it.

ALAN KING

If a Jew breaks a leg he thanks G-d he did not break both legs; if he breaks both, he thanks G-d that he did not break his neck.

SAYING

Psychoanalyst: A Jewish doctor who hates the sight of blood.

Two things grow weaker with the years: teeth and memory.

SAYING

I was in group analysis when I was younger, because I couldn't afford private. I was captain of the latent paranoids softball team. We used to play all the neurotics on Sunday morning; the nailbiters against the bed-wetters!

WOODY ALLEN

To learn from the young is to eat unripe fruit and drink new wine; to learn from the old is to eat ripe fruit and drink old wine.

SAYINGS OF THE FATHERS

For the ignorant, old age is winter; for the learned, it is the harvest.

SAYING

> Four things make a man age prematurely: fear, anger, children and a bad-tempered wife.
>
> MIDRASH: TANHUMA

On Groucho Marx's celebrated TV show *You Bet Your Life*, a Japanese contestant said he was twenty-one.

'Is that in years or in yen?' asked Groucho.

'You don't count age in yen,' said the contestant.

'No?' cried Marx. 'I have a yen to be thirty again!'

Groucho: How old are you, ma'am?
Contestant: I'm approaching forty.
Groucho: From which direction?

Old soldiers never die – they just write their memoirs.

ART BUCHWALD

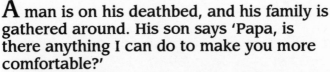

A man is on his deathbed, and his family is gathered around. His son says 'Papa, is there anything I can do to make you more comfortable?'

'I want to taste mom's chopped liver, just once more before I die, please, some chopped liver.'

'OK Pop, I'll get it.' He comes back a moment later.

'Do you have the liver?'

'No, mom said it's for after!'

BILLY CRYSTAL

When he was about seven years old, George Burns found a pair of pince-nez in the street. He loved to wear them because he felt they made him look more mature.

'They belonged to a man of about seventy,' said Burns. 'I used to think that a man of seventy was very old. Now if I meet a man of seventy, I send him out for a glass of water.'

I was always taught to respect my elders and I've now reached the age when I don't have anybody to respect.

GEORGE BURNS

George Burns was discussing his girlfriends, since his wife, Gracie, had died. He did not boast of sexual performance, however and admitted, 'At my age, I'm lucky to have a pulse!'

People think all I have to do is stand up and tell a few jokes. Well, that's not as easy as it looks. Every year it gets to be more of an effort to stand up.

GEORGE BURNS

A Czech, a Pole and a Jew were all sentenced to death in Russia. Each was granted a last wish.

'My last wish is that my ashes are scattered over the grave of Masaryk,' said the Czech.

'And I want my ashes scattered over the grave of Pilsudski,' said the Pole.

'And I want my ashes,' said the Jew, 'scattered over the grave of Comrade Stovinsky.'

'Comrade Stovinsky!' replied the Soviet official. 'But, Comrade Stovinsky isn't dead yet!'

'I know,' replied the Jew, 'but I'm willing to wait!'

Plan for this world as if you expect to live forever; but plan for the hereafter as if you expect to die tomorrow.

IBN GABIROL

On her eightieth birthday, Mrs Bloom decides to write her last will and testament. She goes to see Mr Cohen, her solicitor, and tells him all the financial details: who she wants the money to be left to, who will inherit her estate, her late husband's estate – everything.

Finally she tells her solicitor, 'Although it is forbidden in my religion, I want to be cremated.'

'Are you sure?' said Cohen. 'Won't that upset your family?'

'I'm sorry, but that's my wish and I want it executed. Also, I want my ashes to be scattered over the fountain at Brent Cross Shopping Centre.'

'What!' cried Cohen. 'Are you crazy?'

'Certainly not,' replied Mrs Bloom. 'At least I'll be sure my daughter visits me twice a week!'

———————

Ruth Markowitz went into work one morning, and her boss couldn't fail to notice the big diamond ring on Ruth's right hand.

'That's quite a spectacular diamond you have there, Ruth,' commented her boss.

'Isn't it wonderful? My mother-in-law gave me six hundred pounds before she passed away. She said that when she died I should buy a beautiful stone. So I did!'

Jack Benny: I just can't get over your
youthful appearance. Just look at you: not
a grey hair on your head!
Eddie Cantor: Grey or black, at least it's all
mine!
Jack Benny: So what? I've got hair at home
I haven't even used yet.

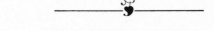

At the funeral of a rich Jewish businessman,
a man stood by the graveside and wept and
sobbed inconsolably. At last a woman
turned to him and asked,
  'Are you a relative of the deceased?'
  'No,' answered the mourner, still sobbing.
  'Then why do you weep?'
  'That's why! !'

There was a pauper who suddenly won the lottery and saw the chance to change his life. Now this man wasn't just a pauper. He was a cripple – very ugly.

So he decided to use his winnings to do something about himself and went to a hospital to see a plastic surgeon and get the complete works. He wanted everything done – hair transplanted, nose straightened, face put right, legs made the same length, even his hunchback straightened out. The doctor told him what it would cost and how long it would take, but his new patient was insistent and he set to work.

For two years he stayed in hospital. Through operation after operation he was in terrible pain. But when it was all over he came out with new teeth, new hair, a new nose – a tall, handsome man. Wallking down the street, for the first time in his life a woman smiled at him. All his life until then people had just turned away. This was the first woman who'd ever looked at him in that way and he went right up to her and asked, 'Would you marry me?' She didn't need a second asking.

So the wedding took place. But right after the reception, as they were leaving for their honeymoon, the bridegroom was knocked down by the reversing wedding car and killed outright.

The minute he got to heaven he went straight to the Almighty and demanded to know, 'Why did you do that to me? After two years of torture getting myself into this shape you have to go and do a thing like that.'

'Who are you?' said the Lord.

'Isaac Cohen.'

'Isaac Cohen?' replied the Almighty. 'I didn't recognize you!'

It's not that I'm afraid to die. I just don't want to be there when it happens.

WOODY ALLEN

To me funerals are like bad movies. They last too long, they're overacted, and the ending is predictable.

GEORGE BURNS

If you begin to think of death you're no longer sure of your life.

SAYING

Ever since dying came into fashion, life hasn't been safe.

SAYING

If someone died and left both sons and daughters: if he left a large estate, the sons inherit it, and the daughters are maintained out of it. But if he left a small estate, the daughters are maintained out of it, and the sons receive nothing.

MISHNAH

Benny Epstein was dying. He had left hospital to die at home with his family around him. One winter night, as a storm was raging and winds howling, Benny called his wife, 'Gertie, Gertie,' he moaned, 'I think the time has come.'

'What?' cried Gertie.

'Dolly, dolly, I'm near to meeting my parents and grandparents and of course the Lord himself.'

'Oh Benny . . .'

'I want to be with a man of the cloth before I pass away. Call Father O'Malley at St Paul's Church.'

'Father O'Malley?' repeated Gertie. 'But darling, Father O'Malley is Catholic! Are you sure you want a Father here? Surely you want me to call Rabbi Greenberg?'

'No, no, no,' said Benny.'You think I'd let the Rabbi come out on a night like this? !'

Three nuclear scientists had been so badly contaminated, there was little hope of saving them. Each was asked to express a dying wish.

'I would like to meet my President and receive the Legion of Honour,' replied the Frenchman.

'I too would like to meet my President and be decorated by him,' answered the American.

'And your request?' the Jew was asked. 'What do you want?'

'A second opinion!'

A man visits his doctor and is told, 'It's cancer. You've got cancer.'

The man, clearly devastated, says, 'I think I'd like a second opinion.'

'Fine,' says the doctor. 'You're ugly as well.'

Life is full of such sadness and sorrow, sometimes I think it's better not to be born at all! But how many people do you meet in a lifetime who were that lucky?

SAYING

As a man enters the world, so he departs.

He enters the world with a cry, and departs with a cry.

He enters the world weeping, and leaves it weeping.

He enters the world with love, and leaves it with love.

He enters the world with a sigh, and leaves it with a sigh.

He enters the world devoid of knowledge, and leaves it devoid of knowledge.

ECCLESIASTES RABBAH

Cyril died, and the first thing he requested when he got up to Heaven was a glimpse of his revered rabbi, who had died a few weeks earlier.

Eventually, G-d gave in, but to Cyril's horror he saw the rabbi sitting with a busty blonde on his lap, playing with his beard.

'Rabbi!' he cried. 'What's happened to you? When you were alive you were a Saint, our leader, how can you *behave* in such a brazen way?'

'You don't understand, my disciple,' replied the rabbi. 'She's not my reward. I'm her punishment.'

Two children were discussing life:

'Do you know what it means to die?' asked one.

'Of course,' said the other. 'First people are born. Then they go to school. Then they go to work. Then they get married. They become mother and father, then grandfather and grandmother. Then they begin to speak Yiddish and then they die.'

The old man was dying, surrounded by his family.

'Are you there, Michael?'

'Yes.'

'And Erwin?'

'Yes.'

'And Ruth?'

'Yes.'

'And Esther?'

'Yes.'

'And Sarah?'

'Yes.'

'And Joseph?'

'Yes.'

'And Miriam?'

'Yes.'

'And David?'

'Yes.'

'Well!' cried the man. 'So who's looking after the shop?'

Seymour: Jack, Jack, I'm dying and before I go, I want you to know that I stole the £150,000. I was the one who leaked those documents and I was the one who was having an affair with your wife all those years.

Jack: Seymour, who do you think gave you the poison?

Yvonne wanted to get in contact with her deceased husband, Hymie, so she visited a medium.

'Ask him how he's doing,' said Yvonne.

'I'm absolutely fine,' replied Hymie.

'Ask him what he's doing. Is he bored? Has he made friends?'

'Tell my wife,' said Hymie to the medium, 'that I'm having a fantastic time. I wake up, have sex and then eat breakfast. Then I have sex again and eat some more, go for a stroll and then have sex just before lunch. Then, after a little siesta, sex again and another bite. Then a stroll before dinner and after dinner it's sex again before it's time to sleep.'

Yvonne couldn't believe it.

'I don't understand! When he was alive he was an extremely fussy eater and he wanted sex about twice a year. How come he's having such a good time?'

Came the reply, 'Well, down there I wasn't a rabbit!'

'**M**orry, Morry, are you there?'

'Renee, can't you see? I'm right next to you?'

'Makes a change. I'm not used to you being home.'

'Come on, bubeleh, you don't expect me to be away when you're dying, do you?'

'Why not? You were away most of the time I was living.'

'Renee, darling, this isn't the time to argue.'

'Ach! Morry, I want you to promise one thing. How many cars are going to the funeral?'

'I don't know. Maybe three or four.'

'Including the hearse?'

'Yes, yes, but I don't want to talk about this now.'

'Well, I do. It's my funeral, so listen. Three cars are plenty. If people want to come, then let them walk. But I want you to promise me . . .'

'Anything, I'll promise you anything, dolly.'

'I want you and my mother to travel together.'

'Me and your mother? I haven't spoken to her for years!'

'I don't care. I want you to promise.'

'All right . . . But I'll tell you something, Renee, it will spoil the day for me!'

The King of Eulogies was Georgie Jessel. Nobody could move an audience like he could. He loved standing up there stirring our emotions, wringing out every tear. That was Jessel at his best. He'd rather be a smash at Forest Lawn than a hit at the London Palladium.

When Al Jolson died, Jessel took it for granted that he would do the eulogy. But twenty-four hours passed and nobody had called him. He became very concerned and telephoned his agent. The agent told him, 'Georgie, I hate to tell you this, but I think they're going with somebody else.'

Jessel said, 'You've got to do something. I've been rehearsing his eulogy for hours, I've got it memorized. Nobody can put Jolie away like I can.' He was so upset that he went over to see Mrs. Jolson. 'Look,' he said,'I've known Al all my life. What's the problem? Am I doing it or am I not?' She started to hesitate and Jessel said, 'If I don't get to do Al's eulogy, I'll never speak to him again.' Anyway, he did the eulogy and it was beautiful.

The next day at the club I saw him, and I said, 'That eulogy you did at the mortuary for Jolson was so touching. You had us all crying like babies. You were just magnificent.' Jessel said,'If you think that was something, you should have caught me at the grave.'

GEORGE BURNS

When the time came for Morrie, Sidney and David to meet their Maker, the three of them arrived together at heaven's gate, where they were greeted in turn by the Angel Gabriel.

'Morrie, by what virtue do you think you're entitled to enter heaven?' asked the Angel.

'Well,' said Morrie, 'I was married to my Sarah for fifty years, she was the only woman in my life, I never went with a woman before I met her, never went with another woman during our fifty years together and never even looked at another woman after she died.'

'You're such a good example,' said the Angel, 'here's a set of keys to the Rolls-Royce over there, so you can drive round heaven in it.'

The Angel turned next to Sidney: 'And what about you?'

'Well, almost the same as Morrie,' said Sidney, 'but I wouldn't lie to you. I say "almost" because once, when I went to Paris, I had a quick fling, but that's the only time I ever made love to a woman other than my wife.'

'Yes,' said the Angel, 'that's pretty good. You won't get a Rolls-Royce for it, but you can take the Jeep over there.'

Last came David and, before the Angel could ask him, he admitted quite frankly that he had been a terrible husband, had committed adultery left, right and centre, and had jumped into bed with tall ones, short ones, fat ones, thin ones – in fact almost any woman that moved. But, on the other hand, David pointed out that out of the tens of millions of pounds he had made, he had given ninety-nine per cent of it to all sorts of charities – Red Cross, Blue Cross, churches, synagogues, orphans, the handicapped – in fact any and every kind of charity.

'That's very unusual,' said the Angel, 'but because of your wanton adultery, all I can give you is a skateboard.'

'Fair enough,' said David, and entered through the gate into heaven. Suddenly he saw the Rolls-Royce parked on the other side with Morrie sitting at the wheel, sobbing his heart out.

'What's the matter, Morrie? You should be the happiest man here, driving a Rolls-Royce round heaven. Why are you crying?'

'I just saw Sarah, my wife,' said Morrie, 'she was on a skateboard.'

Sarah Cohen marched up to the cemetery warden. 'So,' she said.'I've lost my husband's grave. Where is it?'

'What's the name, madam?'

'Nat Cohen.'

'Sorry madam, we've plenty of Cohens but no Nat Cohen. Are you sure that your husband is buried here?'

'Absolutely positive,' cried Sarah. 'Look up our address – 229 Ballards Lane.'

'Aha,' said the warden, looking through his records. 'We have a Cohen at 229 Ballards Lane, but the name is Sarah Cohen.'

'That's right,' replied Sarah. 'That's my husband's grave.'

'What?' asked the bewildered warden.

Sarah shrugged. 'Nu! So, everything's in my name!'

An epitaph

Here lies Nachshon, a man of great renown,
Who won much glory in his native town:
'Twas hunger that killed him, and they let him
die –
They give him statues now, and gaze, and
sigh –
While Nachshon lived, he badly wanted bread,
Now he is gone, he gets a stone instead.

BEN JACOB